# THE
# MEXICAN
# KITCHEN
# GARDEN

JOHN MEEKER

**Andrews McMeel
Publishing**

Kansas City

www.andrewsmcmeel.com

Library of Congress Cataloging-in-Publication Information

Meeker, John, 1932–
    The Mexican kitchen garden  /  John Meeker.
      p.  cm.
    ISBN 0–8362–3257–7 (hd.)
    1. Vegetable gardening—United States.  2. Vegetables—United States.
3. Vegetables—Mexico.  4. Mexican American cookery.  5. Herb gardening.
6. Herbs.  I. Title
SB321.M398  1998
635—dc21                                                              97–28458
                                                                        CIP

*The Mexican Kitchen Garden* is produced by becker&mayer!

Cover photography by Michels Studio/Darren Emmen
Cover design by Trina Stahl and Heidi Baughman
Interior illustrations by Carolyn Vibbert
Interior design by Heidi Baughman
Production and layout by Heidi Baughman and Amy Redmond
Edited by Jennifer Worick

To Setsuko

# CONTENTS

# INTRODUCTION

Experienced cooks demand freshness, and for freshness alone every kitchen ought to have a vegetable garden just outside the door. The kitchen garden is a storehouse of the family's favorite vegetables and fruits. What the cook wants in the kitchen gives the garden its character. A Mexican garden is as identifiable as an English or a French garden. The cactus fence, a sprawling *chayote* vine, beans left to dry in the sun, pepper plants festooned with red, green, and yellow chiles all mark a garden as being Mexican. The three staples—corn, squash, and beans—appear in many traditional American gardens, but when they are accompanied by *tomatillos*, *cilantro*, *epazote*, and *chiles*, the garden is distinctly Mexican.

The gardener can take the following vegetable entries as merely representative of plants that would appear in a Mexican garden. Many vegetables and herbs not included here are also at home in a Mexican kitchen garden. A comprehensive review of Mexican vegetables and herbs is beyond the scope of this book. Regrettably, I have also had to leave out many good gardening and cooking ideas. Chard, for instance, grows year round in Mexico, and

tamales wrapped in chard leaves are especially delicious. To deal excessively with the preparation of garden produce would turn a garden book into a cookbook, so the cooking suggestions are necessarily brief.

The entries that follow are intended to guide the beginner as well as provide a few tips for the experienced gardener. To this end, a Gardening Tips section has been included to help with starting difficult seeds and preparing the soil. With each vegetable entry I have given some suggestions about preparation in the Mexican style, and at the end of the gardening section I have given some recipes that have worked in my kitchen. Finally, at the end of the book I have given some suggestions about further reading for gardeners and cooks interested in the Mexican approach to both topics, along with a list of the best suppliers of seeds and plants.

# THE MOST MEXICAN OF VEGETABLES

# BEANS (Frijoles)

Beans, or *frijoles*, are one of the three chief staples of the Mexican diet, so it is not surprising to find that a wide variety of dried and snap beans are eaten in Mexico, just as in the United States. Because of their keeping qualities, shell beans or "dried beans" are more commonly used than *ejotes* (snap beans), but green beans are no less prized in Mexico than they are in the United States. Mexican cooks use beans in the same ways we use beans—as the basis of soup, salad, or vegetable side dishes. Still, an unadorned tortilla rolled and tucked around a handful of beans is about as Mexican as one can get.

In the garden, happily, beans are among the easiest vegetables to grow. They will tolerate poor soils, dry conditions, and lots of sun, and they will generously reward the gardener who provides well-fertilized ground and a good cycle of irrigation.

## GETTING STARTED

Preparations for working up and improving the soil are the same for dried beans as they are for snap beans. The difference is that dried bean plants will be in the ground longer to allow the pods to mature, dry thoroughly, and last well in storage.

Dried beans take about 100 days to mature and dry out sufficiently, so plant them early in the growing season. Some warm gardening zones will produce three or four harvests successively if, in early spring, beans are sown three weeks apart. Because rain spoils harvests, dried beans do best where the summers are warm and dry.

*The Most Mexican of Vegetables*

Beans grown to be eaten fresh in the pod can be planted at any time during the spring and summer months. Several early varieties of fresh beans mature within fifty days, enabling the gardener to plant beans up to two months before the first autumn frost is expected.

Fresh beans have two kinds of growing habits, allowing us to group them as either bush or pole beans. Bush beans mature faster than pole beans, but pole beans produce a harvest for a longer period. After two to three weeks of harvest, most bush beans do not produce enough new beans to make keeping them worth the space they occupy in the garden. Experienced gardeners like to sow bush beans every two to three weeks to keep them coming through the summer. Pole beans require a structure on which to climb. Poles, vertical strings, nets, and even cornstalks will serve as climbing frames. Five or 6 feet is as high as one wants a trellis; any higher and the beans grow out of reach.

Sow all kinds of beans when the last scheduled spring frost in your area has passed. Space bush beans 3 to 4 inches apart, with 3 feet between rows. Space pole beans 5 to 6 inches apart, with 4 feet between trellises. Beans will not germinate well in cold, dense clay soils. Ground temperature needs to be over 60°F for successful germination. Beans are so easy to germinate that they should be sown directly in

the ground. As a rough guide for sowing depth, plant beans twice as deep as the length of the seed. If beans do not germinate well in your soil and produce lightly, improve their growth and production by adding a legume inoculant with the seeds at planting time. Legume inoculants put nitrogen-fixing bacteria into the soil—bacteria that promote root development and increase yield. Many mail order seed companies that specialize in beans sell inoculants.

## KEEPING IT GOING

Avoid cultivating and harvesting beans when the foliage is wet. Touching wet leaves will spread diseases if there are any present. If a whole bean plant becomes wilted and droops, pull the plant out and destroy it. Keep weeds out of the bean patch. More than most plants, beans tolerate some competition, but rows clear of weeds are bound to produce a better crop and be a source of pride for the gardener.

## PESTS AND DISEASES

Protect against cutworms, if they are a problem, by placing little collars of cardboard (recycled toilet paper cores work well) around the sprouting seedlings. Protect against snails, slugs, and sow bugs by keeping litter picked up and by dusting the sprouting beans with diatomaceous earth. After each watering, the diatomaceous earth will have to be renewed until the beans develop tough stems. (Diatomaceous earth is used in swimming pool filters and can be found in hardware and pool supply stores.) Aphids, mites, and leafhoppers cause curling and discoloring of the leaves. Flea beetles and Mexican bean beetles eat small holes in the leaves and, at their worst, strip the leaves down to a skeleton. Insecticidal

*The Most Mexican of Vegetables*

soap sprays can damage beans, so spray on a test spot to see if the bean plant can survive the type of spray you have selected. If insects threaten the crop, spray a mild pyrethrin–rotenone mix.

Diseases such as bean mosaic—which causes the leaves to yellow, and crinkle, and stunts the plant—are difficult to control. The best solution is to pull up the plants and destroy them. Choose bean varieties that are resistant. Control anthracnose, powdery mildew, and rust with a sulfur spray. Aphids spread viral diseases, so control these rapidly reproducing insects early.

Nematodes cause root damage that results in the plant wilting during the day and recovering at night. Pull out and destroy all plants attacked by nematodes. Before replanting, grow a cover crop of African or French marigolds where you wish to plant beans next time. Organic gardening supply sources have parasitic nematodes that attack and kill the nematodes that prey on plants. Pest-control nematodes should be put into the soil several weeks before replanting.

## HARVEST

Most shell beans are ready for harvest when the pods begin to open, exposing the beans (although not all shell beans do this). The pods of some varieties shatter easily, spilling the beans on the soil. Cutting off plants with a hand clipper when harvesting helps keep pods from shattering.

Allow the beans to finish drying in the sun on a groundsheet. Protect drying beans from rain: Collect them on a groundsheet and carry

them into a sheltered place. Wet beans develop mold and will begin to sprout. The drying period is the critical time during the harvest of shell beans and the prime reason dried beans are best grown in hot, dry climates.

Green beans of both the pole and the bush varieties need picking frequently to keep the plant producing. As beans reach maturity, the plant receives a signal to stop making flowers and to put its energy into making seeds. Pick beans every few days, and pick off and discard the old, mature beans you may have missed on earlier pickings. If saving seeds is the objective, isolate a few plants that have well-formed pods, mark these plants with a strip of cloth to identify them, and treat them as dried beans.

Beans, especially bush beans, crop early, so when the harvest declines, pull them up and plant another crop for late summer or autumn. Good succession crops are radishes, lettuce, and spinach.

Some cooking recommendations might help you enjoy your harvests. Snap beans should never be boiled in water too long—they should still be bright green when served. Depending on the size of the bean, snap beans will be done in 5 minutes (for pods with no seed development) to 12 minutes (for more mature pods). Drain them quickly when a taste test demonstrates they are ready, sprinkle with salt and pepper, and squeeze lime or lemon juice on them before serving. Chile pepper flakes give them a Mexican flavor. When cooking any type of dried beans, do not salt the water initially because it toughens the beans. Add salt to taste after the beans are nearly finished and have become tender. Add *epazote* (the traditional flavoring in soup made from dried black beans) to cooking beans during the last 10 minutes.

*The Most Mexican of Vegetables*

# CACTUS (Nopal)

An emblem of Mexico, prominent on its national flag, is the *nopal,* or what in the United States is called the "prickly pear cactus." Edible parts of cactus are the young tender pads, called *nopales,* and the fruits that form the bases of the flowers, called *tunas*—the prickly pears.

After the spines have been removed, the fleshy green pads are as nutritious and fit to eat as heads of cabbage. Later in the season, the base of each flower, the ovary, ripens and turns from green to red, orange, or yellow—again depending on the variety—and the *tuna* becomes a sweet fruit.

For the cactus grower, all that is needed is a climate in which killing freezes do not occur in the winter. Mature *nopal* plants will take a lot of frost and light freezes. In gardening zones where the odd freeze occurs, an established cactus will lose its pads to frost, but they will come back from the roots if the roots themselves are not frozen.

## GETTING STARTED

Propagation of the *nopal* can be done by seeds, but the fastest method is to cut a fully developed pad from an old growth and plant it cut side down in a pot filled with porous soil. Bury it deeply enough to prevent the pad from falling over. A mixture of gravel, sand, a little garden loam, and perhaps some broken pottery makes a lean soil in which the *nopal* will prosper. Mature plants will grow in heavy clay soils,

but be sure to provide drainage, and keep the soil moist but not soaked. No fertilizer is needed. Keep the pot in filtered sunlight. The *nopal* should be firmly rooted in three months, but give it a full year in the rooting medium before transplanting.

Only if mature cactus cuttings are not available is propagation from seeds recommended. To grow the *nopal* from seed, it is best to sow the seed in a bed especially prepared for it. Use a nursery flat or shallow container filled with a mix of equal parts of sand, peat, and vermiculite. If all of these materials are fresh from the package, there is no need to sterilize the growing medium.

Broadcast the seeds and push them into the soil no deeper than twice their diameter. Keep the soil moist but not soaked. Some growers put a sheet of glass over the seedbed to keep it from drying out. Should you provide a glass cover, keep the seeds from being cooked to death. On sunny days, remove the flat to the shade or cover the glass with a sheet of plywood. All the seeds that are going to sprout will do so within a few weeks. The disadvantage to growing cactus from seed is that it takes three to five years to develop pads large enough for use.

## KEEPING IT GOING

Weeding among cactus plants is best done when the weeds are thin and immature. Larger cactus plants have spines that are tough and really hurt if the gardener makes contact while working around them. Cacti will thrive among weeds, but an untended bed makes a shabby scene. Although weeds will not kill a cactus plant, standing water will. The essential condition for growing cactus is a well-drained bed. If

*The Most Mexican of Vegetables*

poor drainage is evident, dig one or more ditches to carry the water away from the roots of the cactus plants.

## PESTS AND DISEASES

Although there are insects that eat cactus plants, they rarely become a problem for the North American gardener. A pyrethrin–rotenone spray, available in most garden centers, will eliminate the rare insect problem. The most destructive pests for cactus are young boys who find delight in smashing the pads.

## HARVESTING

The best cactus pads for kitchen use come from new spring growth. They are the most tender, most tasty, and most easily rid of their spines. Remove the tiny spines by singeing cactus pads over a flame before slicing them off, or simply use gloves to protect your hands and slice them off with a very sharp knife. Harvest fruity *tunas* when the green turns to red or gold.

Use cactus pads soon after harvest. Store whole or chopped pads for a few days in the refrigerator by bagging them in plastic to preserve their crispness. Limp pads are not as tasty as fresh, crisp ones. After the spines have been removed, cactus pads can be cut into strips, cubed, or used whole. One recipe for whole pads calls for *epazote* leaves, strips of chiles, and a sharp cheese, such as *queso añejo* or cheddar. The pads are sliced open from one edge, stuffed with the cheese, peppers, and herbs, and the stuffed pad is grilled until done. But the best way for beginners to prepare *nopalitos* is detailed in the recipe section of this book (see page 96).

# CHAYOTE

We know the *chayote* by its Mexican name throughout the Southwest, but along the Gulf Coast, *chayote* is called *mirliton* from New World French. The botanical name *Sechium edule* separates this plant from others in the large family of viny vegetables, of which squash, cucumbers, and gourds are members. It has other peculiarities that set it apart, the most prominent of which is its demand for a hot growing season.

Its credentials as a Mexican vegetable are impeccable. The conquistadores found it had long been in use by the Aztecs (the name *chayote* is derived from the Aztec name, *chayohtli*), and Spaniards spread its cultivation throughout the tropics.

Because *chayote* needs a long growing season, attempts to get a harvest north of frost-free zones fail unless the plant is grown under protection. Even then, it may not produce fruit. Even though gardeners in most of the United States may not find it practical or easy to grow, *chayote* is included

*The Most Mexican of Vegetables*

here because many gardeners in the hot, humid zone from Florida to Texas will find it fun to grow and a pleasure to eat.

## GETTING STARTED

*Chayote* wants lots of space, moisture, rich well-drained soil, full sun, warm days and nights, and a day length of twelve hours to bring it to flower. Given those conditions, it will grow quickly, almost visibly, from first sprouts to a rangy vine. Under optimal conditions, the vines can grow over 40 feet in one summer, so provide a frame on which the vine can grow to keep the fruit off the ground. The frame should be substantial, for in the right climate the plant may produce more than fifty *chayotes*, each of which will weigh around half a pound. The weight of the fruit added to the weight of the vines demands that the frame be well constructed. Commercial growers in Mexico space them about 10 feet apart and use heavy wire supported by stout posts.

Fruit production requires the presence of both female and male flowers. A given plant may produce only male flowers, only female flowers, or if you are in luck, both female and male flowers. The determined gardener must therefore plant more than one *chayote* and give some thought to the mathematical probability that three will be enough to produce the required single male and female plants. Once the flowers appear and the plant is found to have all the sexual parts necessary, the other *chayote* vines can be destroyed to save space. One plant will produce more than the average U.S. family may want to eat in a season.

The flowers appear at the leaf axils—where the stem of the leaf joins the vine—just as in other members of the squash and cucumber family. Female flowers are single and whitish green. Male flowers, on the other hand, are smaller, appear as a branching group, and are more chartreuse green than white.

A source of *chayote* seed may be as close as the vegetable bins at the nearest Latin grocery store. In January or February, plant the whole fruit on its side, the narrow stem-end angled upward, in a large pot of loose, rich soil. A paper pot makes it unnecessary to disturb the roots when moving the *chayote* from the pot to the garden. The paper pot will rot in the ground and free the roots, but knock out the bottom and slit the sides of the pot as a precaution against confining the roots. Keep the pot in the dark and the soil moist until shoots appear. After all danger of frost has passed, transfer the pot to the garden. Two or three weeks before setting out the seed, prepare the garden bed by digging in well-composted manure into a 4-foot square for each *chayote* plant. If your soil is heavy and not well drained, prepare raised beds.

## KEEPING IT GOING

Throughout the long growing season, feed the *chayote* vine weekly with manure tea or monthly with side-dressings of composted manure. *Chayote* needs a lot of water to develop properly. Mulching will help conserve water on sandy soils, and providing adequate drainage in clay soils is an absolute requirement.

## PESTS AND DISEASES

*Chayote* suffers from the same problems as those seen in all the squash/cucumber family. In the South, nematodes frequently attack the plant. Good quantities of compost added to the

*The Most Mexican of Vegetables*

soil before planting, the use of marigolds as a companion plant, and inoculating the soil with beneficial nematodes are all effective to a degree.

Heavy mulching not only helps to conserve water but also keeps down cucumber beetles that attack the plants. *Chayote* is more resistant to powdery mildew and bacterial wilt than cucumbers and summer squash.

## HARVESTING

The long days of summer produce the flowers, but fruit develops during the milder periods of heat in late summer and fall. When the *chayote* is ready, the best size is as large as a pear; nevertheless, smaller, less mature fruit is usable. Try cooking the first fruit of the season with the skin on. The more mature the fruit becomes, the tougher the skin.

Color ranges from light green to white. The *chayote* is often somewhat pear-shaped, but flat more than round. The most common type seen in the United States is furrowed on the bottom as if it had been tucked in. In Mexico, other types have soft spines. Cut, rather than pull, the fruits from the vine. They store well under refrigeration for long periods, about as well as summer squash, but like summer squash, they taste best when used fresh.

*Chayote* may be baked or boiled whole; it may be sliced or cubed to be boiled or steamed with flavoring herbs; or it may be sliced and stir-fried. Boiled, the large single seed in each *chayote* is a delicacy in itself. The flesh of the fruit holds up well in cooking, and the taste is roughly like white summer squash. After cooking, it can be cooled, tossed in a vinaigrette sauce, and served with lettuce as an appetizer. It can be the main vegetable in soup or the vegetable addition to a meat casserole. It can appear alone as a side dish, or it can be candied and eaten as a dessert. The flavor of *chayote* goes well with carrots and rice, and it is enhanced by chile, cilantro, and *epazote*.

But that's not all. The tender, growing shoots that first appear in early summer can be snapped off and prepared in the same manner as asparagus. The tender spring leaves can be cooked like spinach, and the tuberous root can be harvested and prepared like potatoes. One can see why a Mexican family would treasure a *chayote* plant in their kitchen garden.

*The Most Mexican of Vegetables*

# CORN (*Maíz*)

Corn—maize or *maíz*—is a Mexican staple along with squash and beans, and like the other two it has its origins as a cultivated plant in southern Mexico and Guatemala. Corn is on the table every day in Mexico, and it appears in song, folklore, and jokes. In the United States, we think of corn as being as American as apple pie, but corn in the form of the tortilla, a product of ground *maíz*, is American in the greater sense of the word: It has been the staff of life in North, Central, and South America for more than a thousand years.

Like the tomato, fresh corn on the cob—especially the sweet varieties—is a celebration of the power of the summer sun. Ancient peoples loved corn fresh from the garden as much as we do, but they, more than we, depended on their harvest to sustain life the year round. Dried in the field, corn can be stored for many years. Keep it dry, and it will be ready for food or ready for planting the next crop. Right out of the bag, however, dried flint corn is tough stuff to chew and digest, and some basic technology is needed to make it edible.

When corn is soaked in limestone water to remove the outer hull of the kernel, the nutritious inner part becomes *nixtamal*, or, as we know it in the United States, hominy. *Nixtamal* ground fine and kept moist becomes *masa*. Shape *masa* into a ball of dough, press it flat, and it becomes the tortilla. *Masa* molded around meat or vegetables and cooked in a wrapping becomes a *tamal*. Today, *masa* is available in groceries throughout the southwestern United Sates as fresh dough, pliable and ready for forming into tortillas or tamales.

Elsewhere, Latin markets stock *masa harina*, a powdered or dry form of *nixtamal* that has better keeping qualities than fresh *masa*.

## GETTING STARTED

Whether the gardener wants fresh corn or dried flint, Indian, or popcorn, preparation and cultivation are the same. Corn is what is called a "heavy feeder." It uses up the nutrients in the soil, especially nitrogen, and needs rich ground to grow a premium crop. Because a corn crop depletes the soil of nitrogen, corn should not be planted from year to year on the same ground. It will use up most of the available nitrogen in the soil in the first year of growing. At least one month before sowing the seed, apply six wheelbarrow loads of horse or cow manure to each 100 feet of row.

Corn will grow on most soils, but poor soils produce an inferior crop. The richer the ground, the better the drainage, and the closer to a slightly acid condition (a pH of 5.5 to 6.5), the bigger the ears and the better tasting your corn will be.

Plant corn when soil temperatures are at least 60°F. Super-sweet varieties—the kind with wrinkled seeds—need warmer soil, 70°F or higher. Cool soil is the main reason for poor germination of any type of corn, but the new sweet var-

*The Most Mexican of Vegetables*

ieties are particularly sensitive to cold soil. Space all types of corn 8 inches between seeds in the row and 2 feet between the rows. Plant in blocks to ensure adequate pollination. In beds, sow seeds on 10- to 12-inch centers. Push the seed down into clay soil about 1 inch deep, and into sandy soil 2 inches deep. In northern climates, plant popcorn, flint, and Indian corn early because they all need a long growing season to mature and dry in the field.

Super-sweet varieties are troublesome to start early because of their tendency to rot in cool soils, so take a few additional steps to guarantee a good crop of incomparable-tasting corn on the cob. Raised beds of clay soil warm up quickly and give a good return for the extra labor of making them. Early in the season, put three seeds in each drill, and later thin the seedlings back to the strongest. As the ground warms up, plant two seeds in each drill. When the soil is truly warm in late spring, plant only one seed per drill. Plant corn in blocks that will produce no more than your family will use, and plant a block every two weeks until eighty days before the first frost is expected. In a well-managed corn patch stalks have a stair-stepped appearance, and the last harvest comes in right before cold kills the plants.

Corn does not transplant well. Any disturbance of the roots causes it to be set back. One early starting method does work well: Sow corn in rich potting soil inside 4-inch peat pots protected by the warmth of a greenhouse. When the roots begin penetrating the peat pots, set them out in the garden. To help the roots escape, cut away one side of the pot without disturbing them.

Corn is pollinated by wind more than by insects, and cross-pollination will occur when two varieties are too close together. Flint corn, for instance, grown near a super-sweet variety will cause the sweet corn to produce inferior-tasting ears. Most home gardens with limited space will do well to stick to one variety.

## KEEPING IT GOING

Corn needs feeding at the 10-inch and 20-inch growth stages. Side-dress with manure lightly scratched into the soil. As an alternative, apply manure tea regularly every ten days until the ears are formed. (Manure tea is made by allowing barnyard manure to steep in water for several days.)

Corn roots are shallow and easily damaged by over-enthusiastic cultivating. Use restraint when hoeing to scratch in manure and to eliminate weeds. Tilling the rows to throw up soil against the base of the cornstalks is an old way to give stalks additional support. In loose, sandy soil, cornstalks may need this extra support to resist strong winds. Removing the suckers from the base of each cornstalk, however, is a waste of time.

Irrigate your corn patch by drip or by flooding in the morning hours. Overhead watering in the afternoon and evening creates wet surfaces that invite pests and diseases.

## PESTS AND DISEASES

Mice and several types of birds will uproot and destroy corn seedlings. Row covers are more effective at deterring birds than scarecrows and swinging aluminum pie plates. Prevent cutworm damage by surrounding each seedling with a ring of cardboard (recycled toilet paper cores will make three rings each). A drop of mineral oil placed on the silks soon after they dry combats earworms.

*The Most Mexican of Vegetables*

Yellowing seedlings indicate that the gardener did not put enough nitrogen into the soil or that the nitrogen is locked up and unavailable to the plant. Water regularly and apply a dilution of fish emulsion to bring the green back into the plants. The condition is usually temporary: Warm weather and rain cause the nitrogen in the soil to be released to the plants.

Smut attacks ears of corn, discoloring and disfiguring them. Early in its development, smut is whitish. As the fungus galls age, they become black and are filled with a black powder that spreads to other ears and infects them. A fungal disease, smut looks either disgusting or delicious, depending on your cultural viewpoint. Experienced gardeners in the United States advise destroying the whole plant as soon as the disease is detected, to prevent its spread. In Mexico, the opposite view holds: Smut is a gift of nature. To Mexicans, what we see as disfigured ears of corn are a delicacy comparable to mushrooms or truffles. The best cookbooks on Mexican food have at least one recipe for *huitlacoche*, the Mexican name for smut-stricken corn. Try not to be put off by the unappetizing color and shape: Think "mushroom," think "truffle," think "exceptional opportunity!"

## HARVESTING

Leave popcorn, flint, and Indian corn in the garden until the stalks and husks have dried. Break the ears from the stalks with a downward twisting motion. If rains have wet the drying corn, bring the corn indoors to finish drying in a warm airy place. Wet and insufficiently dried corn will soon become spoiled with molds.

Harvest sweet corn as the silks become dry and brown. Carefully pull back some of the green husk covering the ear to see if the kernels are fully developed. Break a kernel with a thumbnail to observe the liquid that flows out. If the liquid is clear and watery, the corn is not yet ready for eating. If a kernel bursts with a thin, milky fluid, it is at its optimal sweetness. If thumbnail pressure causes a creamy sluggish liquid or no liquid at all, it is past its prime and most of the sugar will have become starch. On stalks with more than one ear, the topmost ear ripens first.

Fresh corn is neck-and-neck in competition with that well-known summer treat, homegrown tomatoes. There is no more Mexican way to enjoy fresh corn on the cob than to cook it in its green husk. Simply pull back the husks, leaving them attached at the base. Remove the silks, sprinkle with lime juice, salt, and dust with dried chile flakes. Rewrap the husks, tie off with kitchen twine, grill, boil, or microwave, and serve hot in its husks.

*The Most Mexican of Vegetables*

# CUCUMBERS *(Pepinos)*

Cucumbers are another European import to the New World, but through long use in the Mexican kitchen, they have earned their place in the garden. Cucumbers thrive in hot weather, and when eaten they are an anodyne to oppressive heat. Eat cucumbers fresh, uncooked with a little lime juice and chile pepper flakes; make them into salsas; serve them sliced in a peppery vinaigrette; or use them as substitutes for *chayote* in stir-fry dishes.

Although they need care and attention to be at their best, cucumbers are easy to grow. As long as it is provided with a very fertile soil and plenty of water, a skinny vine will produce many times its weight in cucumbers. Considering the amount of energy put into growing it, the cucumber is one of the most rewarding vegetables in the garden.

## GETTING STARTED

Two to three weeks before planting, manure the ground. Put in as much manure as is available, as long as it is fairly well composted and well mixed with garden soil. Plant cucumber seed directly in the ground when the ground is thoroughly warm and all danger of frost is past.

Start cucumbers early by sowing seed in pots of rich potting soil. The larger the pot, the earlier the seed can be started, but an 8-inch pot is the largest size that can be transferred with ease. When transferring the cucumber plants from pot to garden bed, knock out the plant and set in the cucumber seedling with care. If the roots are disturbed, the plant will be stressed, setting it back in its development and wasting the time spent trying to get an early start.

Whether starting seeds in the garden or in pots, push them into the soil to 1 inch deep. In the row, plant two to three seeds 10 to 12 inches apart and thin back to one plant after the seedlings have become 2 inches tall. In the pot, plant two or three seeds and thin back to the strongest single plant. Planting cucumbers in small hills that have been dug and manured is a favored method for some gardeners. Plant four to five seeds per hill, and thin seedlings back to the three strongest plants.

Experienced gardeners make space for other vegetables by providing trellises or nets for the cucumber's sprawling vines. Training cucumber plants to grow upward gives the vines increased air circulation and helps combat powdery mildew. Trellised cucumbers have the additional advantages of being easier to pick and staying cleaner than those that lie on the ground.

## KEEPING IT GOING

Feed cucumber plants every week or ten days with manure tea, or side-dress the plants with composted manure every three weeks. More than most vegetables, cucumbers are sensitive to how much and how frequently they are watered. Rules of watering are pointless, for climate and soil are great variables that make every garden different. It is up to the gardener to determine what his or her cucumbers need. Cucumbers stressed

*The Most Mexican of Vegetables*

from too much or too little water will be bitter. Raised beds seem to be the solution for under- and overwatering compact clay soils. Mixing compost and manure liberally into sandy soil is the solution to the problem of loose soils rapidly losing moisture. Mulches of compost, paper, or black plastic also help conserve water.

## PESTS AND DISEASES

Cucumbers are host to many diseases and pests. Powdery mildew attacks the plants late in the season as the days and nights grow cooler. Elevating plants off the ground helps, but most useful in keeping this disease from taking over is to water either by drip irrigation or by flooding. Overhead watering, especially in the evenings, promotes mildew and other diseases.

Scab, bacterial wilt, and anthracnose are cucumber problems. Scab is a fungus on the fruit that appears first as insect damage and later as gray mold. Bacterial wilt is a disease carried from plant to plant by the cucumber beetle, and it causes the plant to suddenly wilt and die. Anthracnose is a seed-borne fungus that appears first as dark spots on the leaves and later causes the fruit to become dark and drop. The best way to avoid these diseases is to rotate the crops at least every other year. However, if a disease occurs, rotate cucumber plantings every three years. The next best remedy is to dig in lots of compost and manure early in the spring. Healthy plants are less susceptible to bacteria and viruses, and the health of a plant is dependent on the health of the soil. Pull out plants affected by scab, wilt, and anthracnose, and destroy them. Use resistant or tolerant seed varieties next time.

Aphids, spider mites, and various beetles attack cucumber plants. If the plant has a strong leaf structure, remove any affected leaf and destroy it. If leaf removal would denude the plant, spray the leaves with insecticidal soap.

## HARVESTING

Pick cucumbers frequently. Leaving them on the plant to become overly mature and useless is the best way to signal to the plant that it can stop producing because the season is over. Since every cucumber type has its optimal size for picking, no given measurement will fit all—but I prefer picking them smaller rather than larger, no matter what the type. Eat the cucumbers right off the vine as you go about your gardening chores, and you'll find that the smaller ones are crisper, sweeter, and more flavorful. Only the home gardener can serve tiny cucumbers still attached to their flowers as decorations on salads and soups.

Cucumber salsa is a favorite preparation because of its simplicity and freshness. The best cucumbers for salsa are picked before they are fully mature, when the skin is tender and easily digested. Peel them imperfectly, leaving some of the green skin remaining. Chop fine cucumbers, a white onion, green and red chiles, and cilantro, and mix together. Salt to taste and add a squirt of lime juice and a dash of tequila before refrigerating it. Serve the salsa cold after two or three hours of marinating. A spoonful of cucumber salsa with leftover meat or chicken makes a great taco lunch on a hot summer's day.

*The Most Mexican of Vegetables*

# GARLIC (Ajo)

We in the United States, on the whole, tend to be a little shy about appreciating garlic, but after years of being influenced by Italian and Mexican restaurants, more of us are accepting, even demanding, garlic. There is a strong snob factor associated with garlic. Some lovers of the aromatic bulb look down on those who cannot or will not eat it. Take it or leave it, garlic is one of those European transplants that has become an essential ingredient in Mexican cuisine.

## GETTING STARTED

Garlic is, almost without exception, grown from kernels (or cloves) broken from the bulb (or head). Garlic needs a long time in the ground—time to sprout, time to develop a cluster of kernels, and, most important, time to cure in the sunlight. At low elevations and in southern gardening zones, treat garlic as a winter crop, and at high elevations and in the North, handle it as a summer crop. To find an answer to what is South or North, and what is low or high, look to Nature herself. If in winter the soil freezes and heaves, plant early in spring as soon as the ground can be worked. If, on the other hand, your gardening zone has frost at night in the winter, but onions and leeks survive, plant in autumn.

Garlic will endure frost, but it will not live if the bulb becomes frozen. Those who garden in a climate experiencing something between killing frosts and gentle frosts should protect garlic bulbs from the infrequent freeze by mulching with straw or compost. As an illustration of how long garlic takes to form a crop, consider the practice of commercial growers in California. They plant garlic from October to November and harvest in July. California's Mediterranean climate—in which rains start in November and end in May—makes winter an ideal growing period for garlic, and the intense California sunlight dries and cures the crop in the field.

Order garlic sets from seed suppliers, or use cloves from the heads bought at the local grocery store. Seed suppliers have a range of garlic types from which you can choose, and some of their varieties are very close to the red garlic most frequently used in Mexico.

Garlic is tolerant of a wide pH range of soils, from an acid 5.5 to a basic 8.0. Because garlic is going to be in the ground for a long time and because it is in the fertilizer-hungry onion family, prepare the ground well before putting out the sets. Dig down deep and incorporate as much compost, peat, and barn waste as you have the time and energy to till into the soil.

Garlic, like the onion, needs good drainage and does best in loose, sandy soil. Nevertheless, garlic grows well in clay soils if drainage is provided, as, for instance, in raised beds. After preparing the bed, push the garlic sets into the soil about 3 inches deep in sandy loose soil and 2 inches deep in heavier soils. Push each clove down into the soil

*The Most Mexican of Vegetables*

with the root end (the flat end) down and the pointed end up. Space them 3 inches apart in the row and 18 inches apart between rows. In beds, put them on 6-inch centers because getting light down to the bulb is essential for it to develop to full size.

If you're starting garlic in summer, apply a light mulch soon after planting. It is as important that garlic kernels not dry out during their development as it is that they not sit in soggy, poorly drained soil. Planted late in fall, garlic sprouts slowly. Shoots of green should appear within ten days to two weeks.

## KEEPING IT GOING

To develop the largest bulbs, garlic needs a lot of water, fertilizer, and no competition from weeds. Water during rainless periods. Fertilize regularly by applying composted manure as a side-dressing, or give your garlic manure tea every week to ten days.

Keep the necks of the bulbs from becoming heavily covered by soil when side-dressing and cultivating. To ready the mature bulbs for harvesting, make sure they're "high and dry." Soil hilled up around their tops holds in moisture that invites molds to discolor the skin of the bulbs and decreases their storage life.

## PESTS AND DISEASES

Because insects and diseases that afflict it are rare, garlic is well-known among gardeners as a carefree plant. As long as garlic is grown on well-drained, rich soil and rotated every three years, it will be free of pests and soil-born diseases.

## HARVESTING

Well-formed bulbs and tops that are beginning to yellow signal the garlic plant's growth cycle has come to an end. Withhold all water from the plants. The area where the bulb joins the neck of the stalk softens, and the tops lean over.

The objective in harvesting is to have bulbs that will store over a long period of time. Allow the bulbs to continue to ripen in the ground until the soil becomes dry. Turn them out by lifting them with a fork, and allow them to continue to dry in the sunlight. Where skies are clear and the intensity of the sunlight will scald the bulbs, knock off the dirt, bring the bulbs into a well-ventilated shady place, and continue to cure them for several days. Rain damages the crop by encouraging mold.

Garlic may be preserved by pickling, canning, or freezing. Freeze them whole with the papery outside skins on or off. I like to peel the skin from each clove and put them with bay leaves along with red and green chiles in a jar of good-quality olive oil.

Garlic, like chiles, tomatoes, nuts, and cumin, becomes more flavorful when roasted. The roasting also makes the garlic palatable to more sensitive taste buds. Some who find garlic otherwise disagreeable can eat roasted garlic without problems.

# JÍCAMA

It is still listed as yam bean in many garden books, but grocers from New York to San Diego advertise it as jícama (pronounced HEE-ca-ma). *Pachyrhizus erosus* (the botanical name) has traveled from its origins in Central America to the far-flung corners of the tropical world. Jícama is a legume, in the pea and bean family. Other roots known as jícamas south of our border with Mexico are in the morning glory and dahlia families. The jícama most Americans are familiar with has flat, round seeds that resemble overgrown lentils.

Jícama's tuberous root is prepared sliced, grated, or whole, and it is eaten fresh, cooked, baked, or fried. Thin slices of raw jícama hold up well in salads put together with variations of chopped celery, onions, chiles, cilantro, cucumbers, *verdolaga*, spinach, and *quelite*. One very refreshing salad variation is made with jícama and slices of oranges, green chiles, mint leaves, and salt to taste. Added to stir-fry dishes of chicken, peppers, onions, and garlic, jícama imparts a crunchiness and a flavor that make a perfect foil to more strongly flavored vegetables.

## GETTING STARTED

Jícama needs a growing space where the mature vine, which grows long and leafy, can spread up to 20 feet. In short-season gardening zones of the northern United

States, start jícama indoors several weeks before the last freeze is expected. Plants need up to nine months to develop usable tubers. Gardeners in the southern United States who have a long growing season can plant jícamas outside when the ground has warmed enough for planting beans and corn.

Choose that part of the garden that gets the most sun, and dig in compost, wood ash, and manure two to three weeks before sowing the seeds or setting out the transplants. In heavy soils, dig down 18 inches to get compost into the ground and encourage deep root growth. Space 12 inches apart. When planting seeds, sow two or three in a spot, an inch or so apart, and thin out the weakest seedlings after the vines begin to grow. The cost of seed is small compared to the value of your time spent replanting.

## KEEPING IT GOING

Use care in planting tall crops such as pole beans and corn nearby, to avoid shading the vines of the jícama. Jícama grows well next to winter squash and melons, the vines of jícama exceeding these others in length and leaf density. Provide a trellis and keep the vines growing vertically if you need more space for other crops. Some gardeners trim off the pea-like blossoms to direct the plant's energy into developing a larger tuber. I have no evidence to support or deny the validity of this kind of pruning.

In sandy soil, provide a mulch of compost to maintain moisture around the jícama's developing tuber. In clay soil, raised beds provide adequate drainage for the root system. Jícamas favor moist soil, but cannot tolerate standing water.

*The Most Mexican of Vegetables*

## PESTS AND DISEASES

Most diseases that afflict jícama are a result of the roots not being sufficiently drained. A few sucking and chewing insects may occasionally attack jícama leaves and stems, but unless the pests grow in number, let nature take its course. If controls are needed for insects, use an insecticidal soap.

## HARVESTING

There is a lot of vine per plant, but each plant has only one edible tuber. Tubers fresh from the ground are a delicacy that only home gardeners can appreciate, because in most of the United States, jícamas on grocers' shelves have spent several days, if not weeks, in shipment. In Mexico, vendors commonly leave some of the vine and leaves on the tubers to demonstrate their freshness.

Harvest the tuber either ten months after the seeds have been planted or before the first killing frost. To avoid scarring the skin of the tuber, dig it out of the ground carefully. Older tubers that have overwintered in the soil become unappetizingly tough with fiber.

When grown in hot weather, in fertile, well-drained soil, jícama reaches 10 inches across and weighs more than a pound. In most of the United States, those conditions will not prevail. Still, homegrown jícamas, small but fresh from the garden, have a clean, fresh taste that makes them always welcome on the table as an ingredient in salads, snacks, and appetizers, or cooked as a side dish. They store well for many weeks under refrigeration, but they dry out and lose that clean, lightly sweet freshness that makes freshly dug jícamas worth all the time and effort.

# ONIONS (Cebollas)

No kitchen garden—and certainly not a Mexican one—is without onions, whether they be dried bulbs or green scallions, and attempting to cook in the Mexican style without them is unimaginable. Many recipes that use onions call for the white varieties because they hold up better in cooking.

## GETTING STARTED

In addition to their colors ranging from white to red, onions differ in the way they develop their green tops and bulbous bottoms.

Not all onions make a white, brown, yellow, or red bulb. Some, called bunching onions or multipliers, split apart at the base to form several stalks instead of becoming a bulb. It's good to have both forms in the garden, for many recipes call for spring onions or scallions, terms that usually mean young bulbing onions harvested before the bulb has developed.

Both bulbing and bunching onions deserve a place in every kitchen garden. The bulbing types can be stored for long periods and the bunching types are available green throughout the growing season. Furthermore, onions are available for planting in at least one of three forms the year round: as seed, dried bulbs, and as green transplants. The home gardener creates transplants by sowing seeds in a small pot.

Start onions out of doors when soil temperatures are from 55° to 75°F. Onions do best in the sunniest spot in the garden. They prefer soils with a pH of 6.5 to 7.5. They do not tolerate water standing around their roots. Because the soil should be well drained, onions prefer sandy soil, but they will do well in heavy clay in raised beds or when drainage is provided by deep furrows between rows. All soils should be composted heavily and enriched with well-composted manure before sowing seed, setting out transplants, or pushing in bulblet sets.

When sowing seed, plant in furrows ¼-inch deep in heavy soil and ½-inch deep in sandy soil. Press down the soil to make good contact with the seed. Keep the seeds moist until germination occurs. Thin the seedlings 3 to 6 inches apart, depending on the size of bulb expected. To produce bunching onions and green onions from seed, thin to 1 to 2 inches apart.

When putting out transplants, space them according to the anticipated size of the bulb. No thinning will be necessary if your spacings are well planned. The same rule applies to onion sets, which should be put in the ground 1 to 2 inches deep. Onion transplants and sets, however, can also be grown for use as green onions or scallions by spacing them closer together. Bulbing onions cannot take being mulched too heavily; research has revealed that the sun's rays on the bulb help its formation.

## KEEPING IT GOING

Bunching onions and scallions benefit by a mulch of organic material or soil pushed up around the base of the plant. They will grow longer necks resembling small leeks, and the necks will be tender and white if covered gradually as they grow. It is easy to make bunching onions and scallions look like small leeks by mulching up around the plant.

Onions of all kinds need lots of water around their well-drained roots. If your onions go through dry periods, they will lose taste, and the size of the bulb will be reduced. Fertilize frequently with manure tea and side-dressings of manure worked in carefully to avoid damaging the shallow roots. For superior bulb onions, grow them in fertile, moist, well-drained soil. Drought, standing water, and exhausted soil will produce inferior onions. Keep weeds out of the patch; onions do not respond well to competition.

## PEST AND DISEASES

Rotate the crop every three years. Onions need high levels of potassium and nitrogen and a moderate level of phosphorous. Shortages of these elements will result in inferior onions.

Standing water contributes to the invasion of several root diseases. Avoid these by keeping soil moist but well drained.

A fly specific to onions lays its eggs at the base of the plants. The hatched eggs become maggots that enter the earth and eat the onion roots. Yellow cards with sticky surfaces will attract and trap the flies. Mulches of loose organic material also help by preventing them from depositing their

*The Most Mexican of Vegetables*

eggs. Dustings of cayenne pepper around the base of the plants also help to repel the onion maggot fly. Unfortunately, the pepper dust will have to be replaced after watering. Intercropping onions with parsley has been demonstrated to keep down onion fly damage.

Aphids and thrips sometimes attack the green stalks. Daily sprays with a water hose discourage infestations, but should these insects become troublesome, insecticidal soap spray will control them.

## HARVESTING

Bunching onions and scallions are ready for use whenever the plant is large enough to be worth pulling from the soil. When harvesting bunching onions, always leave some bulbs in the ground to multiply and bring on a new crop.

Harvest time is near for bulbing onions when the tops begin to discolor and fall over. Commercial growers sometimes pass a weight over the tops to bend them over and encourage this natural phenomenon. Home growers gently bend the tops over by hand. Do not force the tops if you find that they resist. Bend them too soon and they will break off, limiting the keeping qualities of the bulb.

When the tops are wilted and the necks are loose, lift the onions out of the soil with a garden fork. You can leave them on the ground to cure in the sun or put them elsewhere to cure while the bed is worked up for the next crop. When the necks dry and the tops twist off easily, bag them in open-weave sacks or store them loose in a cool, dark, dry place.

# PEPPERS (Chiles)

*Ristras*—strings of dried red chiles—are so common on the walls of family kitchens and public restaurants that they have become emblematic of Mexican cuisine. Chile peppers are now riding a wave of popularity. Chile Heads, as they call themselves, currently take pride in their knowledge of chiles and in the degree of chile heat they can put through their gastrointestinal tracts. Despite the current interest in Mexican cooking, and perhaps in part because of the ravings of Chile Heads, there is still a lot of caution among the good folk of the United States. When chile is mentioned, the first thing that comes to many minds is the word HOT.

Chiles are, after all, just green or red peppers with a little something extra. The little something extra that makes the difference between hot and sweet is capsaicin. Capsaicin is one of the many alkaloids, such as caffeine, for which humans have acquired a taste. A lot of capsaicin makes a pepper hellishly hot. Just a little capsaicin, and the pepper is mildly hot. If capsaicin is absent entirely, we have what many in the United States would call a user-friendly sweet pepper.

Hot chiles have a complexity that adds interest to Mexican food. There are peppers that give the mildest tickle to the tongue and peppers that impart all

*The Most Mexican of Vegetables*

the pleasures of a surgical procedure without anesthesia. To the connoisseur, there are chiles with an essence of chocolate, of anise, of tobacco, of apricots, of apples. Listening to Chile Heads discourse on the taste of chiles is like hearing gourmets talk about wine.

## GETTING STARTED

For those who do not wish to be dependent on what plants are available at the nursery, growing chiles from seed is not difficult. Time-consuming, yes, requiring attention, yes, but a source of satisfaction, perhaps even fun, for the average green-thumbed gardener. The formula is simple: a sterile growing medium, bottom heat, light, and consistent moisture. More details about growing seed indoors can be found in Gardening Tips (see page 89).

Sow seed indoors eight to ten weeks before the last frost date in your climate zone. Mix vermiculite half-and-half with peat. Screening the growing medium is unnecessary for the chile pepper's large seeds. Sow the seeds no more than ¼-inch deep in the vermiculite–peat mixture. Put the pots on a waterproof tray, which in turn goes on the heating pad. It is very important to prevent the heating pad from getting wet to avoid short circuits.

A temperature range of 70° to 85°F will work. If you can manage it, keep the temperature right at 80°F. In about ten days, the chile pepper seeds will have sprouted. After the seedlings develop their first true leaves, they can be picked off the rooting medium and transferred to 4-inch pots. By the time they develop the look of characteristic pepper plants—four or five leaves on a healthy central stem—feed them weekly with a dilute mixture of fish fertilizer.

Put chile peppers out in the garden when the soil warms to 65° to 75°F. Gardeners in whimsical-weather zones protect chiles with cloches or water-filled plastic jackets, or they cover them at night with caps. Space them about 18 inches apart in rows, with the rows 2 feet apart. In beds, space them on 18-inch centers. Chile peppers develop long, rangy branches that later grow heavy with fruit. Put wire tomato cages over them to keep the branches in bounds and to support the fruit.

Compost and enrich the soil with rotted manure, but soils that are too richly fertilized will cause more growth of stem and leaf, and fruit production will suffer. Chile peppers want to be well drained, so raised beds are a solution where the soil is heavy clay. On sandy, porous soils, compost helps to retain moisture and plastic mulches will keep moisture in the ground.

## KEEPING IT GOING

Feed chile peppers every week through the growing season with a dilute solution of manure tea. As the summer sun gets hotter, the maturing fruit is sometimes subject to sun-scald. Prevent the fruit from burning by covering the plants on the west side with floating row covers made of polyethylene.

## PESTS AND DISEASES

If your chile plants are troubled by sucking insects, such as spider mites, thrips, and aphids, spray with a mild solution of insecticidal soap. If troubled by caterpillars, spray with a solution of Bt *(Bacillus thuringiensis)*. Ordinarily, the fruit of chile peppers is not much troubled by pests, but when putting

*The Most Mexican of Vegetables*

out the baby pepper plants, make a cardboard ring around the base of the plants to repel cutworms. A range of mosaic viruses attack pepper plants and chiles, so choose varieties resistant to viruses.

## HARVESTING

Harvest chile peppers as they develop walls thick enough for use. Many varieties, such as the *manzano*, are picked green. The New Mexico and Anaheim varieties are picked green and red. Many of the best chiles in Mexico are left on the plant to develop thick walls, change their color from green to orange or red, and develop their full flavor. Still, there is no rule that says one cannot use any chile while it is still green for making chile verde early in the season.

No matter how macho you claim to be, use caution when handling the hottest varieties. What is tolerable in the gut is intolerable around the mucous areas of the mouth and eyes. Until you are used to handling the hot varieties and know what you can get away with, use gloves and wash thoroughly after handling chiles.

Dry, can, or pickle your chile crop. Canned and pickled chiles will taste different from the same variety of chile eaten fresh. Of course, they can be frozen whole on the stems, or roasted—seeds and stems removed—and frozen in compact units of prepared chiles. Stringing them up in the summer sunlight is the traditional method for preserving them in colorful *ristras*, but this method is best used in the rainless Southwest. In areas where humidity is high and the sunlight is not strong, dry chiles in a vegetable dryer.

# SQUASHES and PUMPKINS (Calabazas)

The word *calabaza* refers to all the pumpkins, gourds, marrows, and squashes alike, which for centuries were cultivated in Mexico for their seeds, for their flesh, and as gourds, dried for use as containers. Long before the Aztecs, life in middle America was sustained by the three staples—beans, corn, and *calabazas*.

Mexican winter squashes probably vary more widely in appearance and taste than ours do. *Calabacitas* or summer squash, such as our yellow crookneck and zucchini, are used in soups, combined with corn and peppers in vegetable stews, and prepared much as we use them here. Winter squash is used for fillings in a wide range of dishes, from *tamales* to desserts.

## GETTING STARTED

Winter and summer squash require the same preparation. Winter squash take up more room, and summer squash mature quicker and are ready for harvest sooner. The gardener who plants winter squash must plan with time and space in mind. Winter squash need four months of frost-free growing time to be ready for harvest, and they need a lot of space in which to sprawl.

*The Most Mexican of Vegetables*

Viny types such as pumpkin can be raised up by using lath or net trellises, but the labor needed for tying up the vines and providing support for the fruit is more than most gardeners think worthwhile. Winter squash do not demand as much sunlight as many summer vegetables; hence they can be run along a fence or be in the partial shade of cornstalks.

Whether the garden is sandy or clay, a raised bed of composted soil makes an ideal site on which to grow winter squash. Prepare the ground by adding as much rotted manure and compost as you can. Seedlings will be burned by chemical fertilizers and too much uncomposted manure, but it is difficult to imagine a soil so rich in rotted manure that winter squash would suffer.

Space sprawling plants such as pumpkins 6 to 8 feet apart. Hubbard and other more compact varieties want 4 feet between plants. Space compact growers such as acorn and butternut 3 feet apart. Plant three to five seeds twice as deep as the length of the seed. When they develop their true leaves, thin back to two of the strongest seedlings. Winter squash may be grown in rows or, if you are satisfied with less production and smaller fruit, in large containers.

Transplant shock will hold back development of any plant, but winter squash will transplant easily with a minimum of care. If gardening in a northerly zone demands an early start, then sow seeds in peat pots four weeks before the last frost and keep in a protected place. Peat pots allow the root ball to be transplanted whole without disturbing the roots.

Where summer rains are absent or infrequent, as on much of the West Coast, provide a mulch of black plastic over a drip irrigation system. If that is too much trouble, bury around the squash seedlings two or three empty coffee cans with their bottoms pierced. Water and feed the squash through these reservoirs. A mulch of loose material—straw, rice hulls, unfinished compost—also serves to keep moisture around the roots.

Summer squash is more popular than winter squash among amateur gardeners because it takes up less room and brings a quick harvest. Plant seedlings 2 to 3 feet apart in rows, or use the same distance to center spacings in a bed. Provide the same soil conditions, fertilizer, and watering as recommended for winter squash. In zones with long growing seasons, a second—and sometimes a third—planting of summer squash keeps them coming through the summer and fall. Sow fewer seeds, make succession plantings every six weeks, and avoid the glut of zucchini or yellow crooknecks that becomes a burden on the cook and the neighborhood.

## KEEPING IT GOING

All of the *calabaza* family hungers for fertility and rewards the gardener who feeds them. Fertilize every week with a gallon of manure tea. After the plants have become well established but before they sprawl, work in a side-dressing of manure about 18 inches from the base of the plant.

When satisfied with the number of fruit sets on winter squash, start pinching off female flowers to direct growth into increasing the size of the remaining fruit. These female flowers—as well as male flowers—can be harvested and prepared in soups, salads, and various main dishes. Taking female flowers, however, limits the plant's production.

*The Most Mexican of Vegetables*

Harvest summer squash early and regularly to keep the plant producing.

## PESTS AND DISEASES

Centuries of *calabaza* cultivation by Native Americans testify to the plants' hardiness and ability to withstand pests and diseases, as well as indifferent gardeners. Still, problems do occur. Place rings of cardboard around seedlings as soon as they appear, to prevent cutworms from mowing them down. Use wire screens, nylon net, or floating row covers to prevent jays and crows from digging up the seeds and eating the seedlings.

Combat squash bugs, cucumber beetles, and aphids with sprays of insecticidal soap. Squash borers are more difficult. To combat these maggot-like worms that tunnel into the base of the plant and along the stems, plant early. This allows the plants to build up tissue strength to resist the pests. Rotenone sprays at the base of the plant will kill the larvae before they chew their way inside. Once squash borers are located in the stems, slit the stem, remove the borer, and bury the stem where it has been cut. Control other bugs and chewing beetles by picking them off by hand.

All *calabazas* are susceptible to powdery mildew. Space seedlings to provide good ventilation between plants, and clean up all dead squash material from around the plants. Water from below instead of overhead, and water early in the morning instead of late in the evening. Late in the season, apply fungicidal soap to combat mildew.

## HARVESTING

When your thumbnail cannot easily penetrate its skin, winter squash is ready for harvest. Cut the vine about 2 inches away from the squash. Breaking the squash off the vine can damage the flesh and invite rot. Despite the well-remembered line about "frost on the pumpkin," harvest winter squash before they are touched by frost and they'll last longer in storage. Try harvesting some of your winter squash when they are finger-size, young, and tender. They cook up as nicely as summer squash and have as good a taste.

Summer squash is prime for harvest when the squash has reached its pictured shape and color and a thumbnail easily penetrates the skin. Cylindrical summer squash such as zucchini taste best when they are 4 to 7 inches long. Flat scallop and spherical types taste best when they are around 4 inches in diameter. Despite the endurance of the spurious bromide that bigger is better, sweetness and flavor of summer squash are best when they are small. Probably the most common mistake beginners make is to allow summer squash vines to put their energy into making large, inedible fruit. Experienced kitchen gardeners never sacrifice taste for size.

Harvest the blossoms of summer and winter squashes and pumpkins early in the morning when the blossoms have just opened. At that time they are at their most tender and fragrant. Prepare flowers for eating by pinching back the stem of the flower to the point where it is most tender, about 2 inches under the calyx. The sepals are the green tough parts that are just below the flower petals. Strip off the sepals, pulling them down just as one would take the strings off green beans. Squash blossoms with squash and corn in combination make one of the world's outstanding soups.

*The Most Mexican of Vegetables*

# TOMATOES *(Tomates)*

The tomato needs no lengthy introduction. All the world loves this vegetable, which has its beginnings in Central America. Above all others, the tomato is the one vegetable for which all Americans find a place in the garden. In Mexico, tomatoes are the main ingredient of sauces and salsas.

## GETTING STARTED

Every gardener should know how to start tomatoes from seed. By growing bedding plants from seeds, we have the advantage of choosing tomatoes that tolerate cool conditions. By starting from seeds we can select specialty types—the extra large, the extra sweet, the extra early, or the extra late. We can choose exactly what we want—big slicers for sandwiches or orange paste types for sauces. From seed we can grow tomatoes that have been bred to resist the pernicious diseases that may be a problem in our garden. Dedicated gardeners do not have to accept what is available from the nursery. The benefits of growing from seed are compelling, and the job is easier than it first appears. Directions for growing tomatoes and other seeds are detailed in Gardening Tips (see page 89).

There are two types of tomato plants, different in the kind of growth they put out and in the fruit production of the plant. The determinate type of tomato is bred to be a field tomato for large growers. Determinate tomatoes grow bushy, and all the fruit ripens at about the same time. They tend to be tough fruit made for scooping up and processing with a machine. Indeterminate tomato plants become taller, more viny, and produce ripening fruit over a longer period of time. Home gardeners with the time to put up tomato cages or trellises or to train the plants on poles, favor indeterminate tomatoes because they produce over the length of the summer season. A bushy indeterminate tomato has been produced for those home gardeners who do not want to train the indeterminate types.

Put out tomato plants when the soil is warmed above 65°F. Space determinate bushy tomatoes about 24 inches apart. Space indeterminate tomatoes to be trained on stakes or trellises from 18 to 24 inches apart and those that are going to be caged at about 36 inches apart. Make 3-foot spaces between rows of all types of tomatoes. Even when the seeds have been started in the windowsill greenhouse eight to ten weeks before the last frost, the climate is sometimes still cool. Fortunately, tomatoes can be potted up from successively smaller to larger containers without setting back their growth or the development of fruit. Be attentive to potted plants' need for regular feeding by giving them a dilute solution of fish emulsion every two weeks. Keep the roots from getting pot-bound. At intervals, knock a sample rootball out of the pot to check root development. A lot of white roots along the pot sides indicates that the plant should be potted up immediately.

Pot them up from seedlings to larger plants using a mixture of equal parts rich garden soil, compost, and peat. Keep

*The Most Mexican of Vegetables*

the pots in a sunny and warm spot during the day, and, depending on night temperatures, bring them indoors or provide protection from cold air and wind.

As an alternative to successively potting up the tomatoes, they can be put out in the garden soil with some protection. One common protective covering is a plastic skirt that can be filled with water that heats up during daylight hours and keeps the plant warm when the temperature drops at night. Cloches of plastic or glass often have to be taken off or opened during the day to keep the heat buildup from cooking the plant. A combination of cloches and a heat-absorbing black plastic ground cover is a good way to get tomatoes off to an early start. Using these methods to protect cold-tender tomato plants, many gardeners extend their season by starting early.

Tomatoes should be planted in good soil, but not soil high in nitrogen. They want phosphorous, small amounts of potassium and moderate amounts of nitrogen. The recommended soil pH for tomatoes is 6.0 or slightly higher. Ground that was manured heavily in the previous growing

season is ideal for planting tomatoes. Use your best finished compost if you want to improve the tilth of the soil, but do not use manure on tomatoes or they will produce vine to the loss of fruit. To avoid viral and fungal diseases, do not plant tomatoes on ground where eggplants, peppers, potatoes, or other tomatoes have been grown in the last three years.

Plant tomatoes in the sunniest part of the garden. Tomatoes need a minimum of six hours a day of sunlight. On sandy ground, compost mulches help by keeping moisture in the soil near the roots. At the end of the season, the gardener who lays down a thick mulch will find that the roots of the tomatoes have intertwined and penetrated the mulch. On heavy clay soils, use a thinner mulch and provide drainage either by raising the beds or by creating a drainage trench.

When setting out the tomato plants, dig deeply enough to bury the plant to the top set of leaves. Pinch off branches and leaves that will be buried. Roots will develop at these junctures and the plant will be healthier. When you set out large potted plants, lay the rootball in horizontally instead of digging an extremely deep vertical hole. Even on large plants, new roots will develop along the buried stem.

## KEEPING IT GOING

Tomatoes fed by high-nitrogen fertilizers will produce more vine and leaf than fruit. Side-dressings of bone meal and kelp soon after planting time will provide an adequate supply of phosphorous and potassium during the growing season. Manure tea or dilute fish emulsion will keep the plants green without overdoing the nitrogen.

*The Most Mexican of Vegetables*

Indeterminate types can be left alone inside their cages, but on a trellis some support is needed. Use a soft cloth tie such as old toweling or cast-off panty hose.

Keep the roots moist but not sitting in water. Mulches help keep moisture near the roots, especially helpful on sandy soil. A proven method of watering is to run drip irrigation under black plastic cover. Plants that dry out will suffer blossom drop and stop producing fruit. Sudden onsets of cool weather, or—the other extreme—hot weather, will stop fruit production and cause blossom drop. Where sun is intense and fruit is exposed, cover the plants with floating row covers to protect fruit from sunscald.

## PESTS AND DISEASES

Tomatoes are susceptible to a wide range of diseases and pests. The best way to deal with many tomato diseases is to practice good management. Avoid planting tomatoes where eggplants, peppers, potatoes, or other tomatoes have been planted in previous years. The recommended rotation of this family of crops is three to five years between plantings. Soil should be well drained, yet able to hold moisture, and it should be rich in calcium and phosphorous. Prevention of a wide range of diseases is best practiced by choosing tomatoes that are resistant to fungi and viruses to which this plant is susceptible.

Letters following the names of varieties are keys to their resistance characteristics. The letter V designates that the plant has resistance to verticillium wilt, F means resistance to fusarium wilt, T indicates resistance to tobacco mosaic disease, and N notes resistance to root nematodes. Because home gardeners have only a few tomatoes growing at a time, it is a good idea to get varieties resistant to as many problems as possible. It would be a shame to lose the whole summer crop to some virus you never suspected until it was too late. Fortunately, many new varieties of tomatoes have these resistant characteristics bred into them.

Young tomato plants are also frequently lost to cutworms. Protect them by simply encircling the seedlings with cardboard rings the same day they are put out. More mature plants that have been potted up do not need this protection. Apply insecticidal soap early when whiteflies, aphids, leaf hoppers, and spider mites are detected. Chewing insects such as cabbage loopers, corn earworms, and tomato hornworms are controlled by periodic sprays of Bt *(Bacillus thuringiensis)*. Bt works only against caterpillars and is harmless to people and pets. Colorado potato beetles, stink bugs, and cucumber beetles are less of a problem. Handpick these insects early in the morning before the sunlight warms them and makes them evasive.

Blossom end rot spoils fruit by making a brown soft spot at the end of the tomato. Calcium unavailable in the soil is the cause. Add gypsum when preparing the soil for planting in the spring. If the plants have become established before you discover the problem, spray the leaves with a seaweed extract. Blossom end rot is made worse by uneven watering, high salt levels, or by too much nitrogen fertilizer in the soil.

Water tomato plants from below, as is done by drip irrigation. Overhead watering, especially at the end of the day, leaves the foliage wet for long periods, making conditions inviting to pests and diseases.

## HARVESTING

Determinate varieties are bred to be harvested at one time; however, we do not live in a perfect world, and even determinate varieties produce tomatoes that ripen over a period of days. A noticeable decline in the vigor of the plant and in the color of most of the fruit indicates that it is at the end of its life cycle.

Indeterminate varieties produce tomatoes until cold weather finally kills the plant. Leave the fruit on the plant until ripe to get the sweetest tomatoes. Remove damaged and poorly formed fruit before they ripen, to keep the plant's energy directed toward developing more usable tomatoes. Dispose of all fallen and rotting fruit to deny homes to pests and diseases.

Salsa *fresca* is one of summer's treats. In Mexico, it is enjoyed almost year round, but here in the United States the best is made only in the summer, when tomatoes are red and fully ripened on the vine. The recipe for salsa *fresca* is in the recipe section of this book (see page 104), and it is a universal favorite among those fond of Mexican food.

# HUSK TOMATOES
## (Tomates Verdes or Tomatillos)

*Tomatillo* seems to be the name that has stuck in the United States. Seed companies and grocers on both the East Coast and the West Coast now advertise what used to be called the husk tomato under the northern Mexican name *tomatillo*. In southern Mexico, *tomate verde*, or green tomato, is the more commonly used name, although it should be made clear that green tomatoes are not adequate substitutes for the taste of *tomatillos*. *Tomatillos* have just the right mix of sweet and sour taste that makes them essential in green taco sauce, or salsa *verde*.

## GETTING STARTED

When the ground has warmed up sufficiently for you to put in warm-weather plants such as tomatoes and peppers, sow *tomatillo* seed directly in the garden soil. In clay soil, cover the seed by about ¼ inch, and in sandy soil, cover the seed by about ½ inch. Distance the plants from each other by 18 to 24 inches. *Tomatillos* need about seventy-five to 120 days to produce usable fruit. As with most vegetables, variations in days to harvest depend on weather factors.

Get an early start in warm-weather zones by starting seed in six-pack cells of good garden soil, four to six weeks before the ground has warmed up. In cooler zones, start them on a windowsill four weeks before the last frost. Like tomatoes and peppers, *tomatillos* can be potted up from one size of growing container to another. However, for a family of four, all crazy about Mexican food, four vigorous *tomatillo*

*The Most Mexican of Vegetables*

plants will produce enough fruit for a summer, with leftovers for canning and freezing.

Even though *tomatillos* are not heavy feeders and will tough it out on lean soils, amendments of compost to both clay and sandy soils improve the crop.

## KEEPING IT GOING

Because the growth habits of *tomatillos* are the same as those of viny tomatoes, they do well when kept in bounds by a tomato cage. Otherwise, *tomatillo* plants sprawl across other plants and get underfoot. Place the cages early, for *tomatillos* are rapid growers and the sprawling vines need pulling into the wire cages every other day.

## PESTS AND DISEASES

Protect young *tomatillo* plants from cutworms by making a cardboard ring around the base of the seedlings when they come up. Protect them from slugs and snails by keeping the garden clear of litter and rotting vegetation. Dust plants with diatomaceous earth to repel crawling insects. *Tomatillos* are wonderfully free of most of the diseases that afflict tomatoes.

## HARVEST

The *tomatillo* has a small yellow flower on a calyx that expands and covers the fruit like a paper wrapper. A yellowish green tomato-like fruit will develop inside this husk. Well-developed fruit should be around 2 inches in diameter—about the size of a walnut—but smaller *tomatillos* are usable. The plant will produce edible *tomatillos* until cold weather kills it. In warm zones, fruit left on the ground will be transformed the next spring into many new *tomatillo* seedlings.

The condition of the husk indicates fruit quality. When the husk is dry and brownish yet fresh-looking, the fruit is ready for harvest. The husk should not be dry and shriveled. Overripe fruit that has become translucent yellow or purplish does not make salsa *verde* with the taste that aficionados demand.

Still, overripe fruit is usable in other dishes, especially in a mixed salad. Sliced *tomatillos*, cucumbers, onions, and tomatoes, fresh from the garden and marinated in a vinaigrette sauce, make an appetizing and healthy way to begin a Mexican dinner.

*Tomatillos* stored at 35° to 45°F last for a period of two weeks if the fruit has the husks removed and is kept in plastic bags. Recipes for canning green tomatoes will also work to put up *tomatillos*. They can also be preserved by removing the husks, dropping them whole into a plastic storage bag, and freezing them.

# THE MOST
# MEXICAN OF
# HERBS

# AMARANTH (Quelite)

This potherb is known the world over as a delectable hot-weather vegetable green. North Americans do not much use amaranth as a vegetable, but in India, China, Africa, Mexico, and the Andes, people like this plant's leaves for salads and cooked greens and its seeds for grain. Several varieties are available to American gardeners. Only the botanical names keep the various kinds sorted out. *Amaranthus retroflexus* is best known as a weed in North America, where it is called by the unlovely name of pigweed. *A. tricolor*, also *A. gangeticus*, is often sold under the name of Joseph's coat or *tampala*, its name in India, or by its Chinese name, *hinn choy*. The true Mexican varieties of this breed are *A. hypochondriacus* and *A. cruentus*. *A. hypochondriacus* is sold in America as black leaf and green leaf amaranth. *A. cruentus* comes from northern Mexico, where it is known in Mexican Spanish as *quelite* and sold here in the United States as Mayo Red. The Mexican varieties are cultivated as a grain crop as well as for their first tender spring leaves. As soon as the soil warms in spring, it sprouts easily in the worst soil. It grows quickly in warm weather; the leaves toughen as they mature and the tops produce prolific seedheads.

## GETTING STARTED

Amaranth seed is very small but vigorous. Sow seeds ⅛-inch deep in heavy soil and ¼-inch deep in sandy soil. Tamp them down to make the seeds come into contact with the soil. Space the seed about 2 inches apart for greens and 6 inches apart for producing seed. Start with the closer spacing, thin back, and use the greens. Allow the remainder to produce seedheads. Make rows 8 to 10 inches apart. As an alternative to planting in rows, scatter the seed on a bed. Whether grown in rows or beds, use the first tender thinnings for salad greens. Use thinnings from larger growth for cooked greens, and thin the remainder to 10-inch centers for seed production.

Amaranth will grow on the poorest soil in drought conditions, but to get the most succulent plants and the best leaf production, work compost and manure into the soil before sowing the seed, just as you would for heavy feeders such as cabbage or broccoli. Amaranth will germinate in cool ground, but warm soil will cause it to germinate rapidly and grow fast.

For earlier starts, begin amaranth in small pots and, as the plants become larger, either pot them up or transplant them to the garden. Amaranth is one of the few rapidly growing vegetables that transplant and pot up without their development being retarded. Like the group of vegetables called potherbs, amaranth can be grown in a container through its entire life. Give it a big container and rich soil if you're growing it for greens.

## KEEPING IT GOING

Fortunately, amaranth needs little soil improvement after the starting beds have been prepared. It will undergo drought without failing, but water it regularly for better leaf and seed production.

## PESTS AND DISEASES

A few leaf-chewing pests, such as flea beetles, will make holes in the leaves. Whiteflies, aphids, and some caterpillars also attack the leaves.

## HARVESTING

Use earliest thinnings and most tender tip growths as salad. As the leaves age, they become less tender, but no more so than other spinach substitutes such as chard, beet tops, and New Zealand spinach. For a cooked side dish of amaranth leaves, take cuttings from the tops and the tips of side branches. Trimming from the top of the central stalk causes the plant to grow bushy and delays formation of the seed stalk.

To harvest the grain, wait until the seeds begin to fall from the heads when they're shaken. The seeds do not all ripen at once. Knock them into a bucket during the first harvests, and when the last of the seeds become ripe, cut the heads and shake the seeds onto a ground cloth. Threshing and winnowing them by hand is not difficult. The interior seeds easily come free of the hull. Use the seeds for their special nutty flavor in muffins, whole wheat bread, and pancakes. A little experimentation with honey and popped amaranth seeds will allow you to formulate a candy considered a delicacy in Mexico. Sprouted seeds give salads a special taste that cannot be duplicated by sprouts of other seeds.

# CORIANDER (Cilantro)

Recently in the vegetable sections of the grocery store, the old name Chinese parsley has given way to the Mexican name, cilantro. This is another of those easy-to-grow and handy-to-have herbs in the garden. Cilantro is the name usually given to the leaves of the fresh potherb and coriander is the name usually applied to the seeds. The green leaves and dried seed are the same plant, *Coriandrum sativum*.

It is an annual that in hot weather reaches maturity rapidly and bolts to seed. In hot gardening zones, keep cilantro in the garden by planting on the shady side of the house, and plant a new bunch, six to twelve seeds, every three weeks.

You will need cilantro plants throughout the growing season if you are serious about Mexican cooking, for fresh cilantro gives a flavor and smell that cannot be duplicated by parsley or other herbs. Cilantro is an essential element in the preparation of salsa *fresca*.

## GETTING STARTED

As soon as the soil can be worked in the spring, and through the summer, sow cilantro seed ½-inch deep in sandy soil and ¼-inch deep in clay soil. Cilantro is a composite seed that produces two or four plants per seed. Gardening books that recommend 8- to 10-inch spacing of plants have in mind the bushy

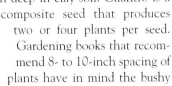

winter growth of cilantro. Although plants grown in summer quickly bolt, they produce useful foliage for a week or more before putting up a seed stalk. The fringy leaves on the leaf-stalk are also useful as cooked greens.

Some seed houses claim to offer seed that is slower to bolt in hot weather. I have grown cilantro during summer days that regularly exceeded 100°F, and I cannot say, after many attempts with different sources of seed, that the so-called slow-bolt cilantro has any significant resistance to bolting. The best method remains successive planting every three weeks.

Cilantro takes a long time to germinate. However, you must keep the bed moist. Allowing germinating cilantro seed to dry out is fatal to success. A light mulch will help. The seed does not transplant well because it has a long tap-root, like others in the parsley and carrot family.

## KEEPING IT GOING

Prepare a rich bed for cilantro in the beginning, and you will not have to attend to it afterward. Stress from competing weeds will hasten bolting, as will drought. Eliminate the competition and keep the roots wet but not standing in water.

## PESTS AND DISEASES

Whiteflies, aphids, and thrips will attack the leaves to some extent, but they are seldom a serious problem. Snails and slugs will mow down the tender seedlings, if given a chance. After the plants are established, these mollusks seem to be uninterested in cilantro. When cilantro flowers, it attracts many species of predatory wasps. Since allowing cilantro to flower in my garden, I have been little troubled by horn-

*The Most Mexican of Herbs*

worms, cabbage loopers, and other caterpillars. I credit the cilantro flower's ability to attract the tiny wasps that lay eggs that feed on the caterpillars as the cause of the near elimination of these pests.

## HARVESTING

Take leaves from cilantro at any time after the first true leaves have developed. The small thinnings are also useful in the kitchen, even though the pungent flavor of the plant increases with maturity. To extend the usefulness of cilantro that has bolted, pull the plants whole from the soil, wash off the roots and immerse them in a jar of water, cover the green tops with a plastic bag, and keep the plants in the refrigerator. Drying cilantro leaves is practical, but to get superior flavor and color from cilantro beyond the growing season, wash, chop, and freeze the leaves and stems in sealed plastic bags. Mexican recipes call for both seeds and fresh green cilantro leaves. To harvest seed from your own garden, simply allow the flower heads to mature. They will change from grayish green to light brown as they dry. Rub the seeds free of the flower stalks on which they have grown. Store them in a tight container in a cool, dry place. The best Mexican food recipes that call for cilantro seeds recommend toasting before grinding to bring out the flavor.

Cilantro has all the applications that parsley has in European cooking. Use it chopped in sauces and soups. Chop tomatoes, cucumber, and cilantro together to make a simple summer salad, and substitute cilantro for parsley as a garnish on meat dishes and fish. Salsa variations made with onions, tomatoes, chiles, and cilantro are endless.

# CUMIN (*Comino*)

Cumin (*Cuminum cyminum*) is indigenous not to Mexico but to the Middle East, from whence it has spread to flavor the cookery of the world. Nevertheless, Mexican food would not be the same without it. Use it in rice dishes, soups, and sauces. When using it, do not overlook toasting to bring out the flavors as the Mexican cooks do with most seeds. Unlike others in the carrot/parsley family, cumin is not an easy seed to start. Yet in climates and soils where it finds a good home, it will reseed itself and come back year after year. It is a low-growing annual—usually 6 to 18 inches high—that wants warm soil and warm weather to germinate successfully.

## GETTING STARTED

Sow the seeds in a container or in the ground in loose, well-drained soil. In cool climates, bottom heat will help containers of cumin seed to germinate. In northern climates, sow cumin seed in a hotbed under glass and transfer later to a sunny spot in the garden. Cover the seeds to no more than ¼ inch and keep them moist until they germinate.

## KEEPING IT GOING

The plants grow vigorously after the first true leaves develop. The long and narrow deep green leaves may have some application in the kitchen, but the seeds are what we want for Mexican cooking. After the little clusters of white-pink flowers blossom in about three months, the

*The Most Mexican of Herbs*

carrotlike umbels begin to set seed. Cold weather will set back seed development, and frost will kill the plants.

## PESTS AND DISEASES

Spray the rare insect infestation with an insecticidal soap.

## HARVESTING

The seeds are oblong, ⅛-inch wide by ¼-inch long. Before harvesting, allow the seeds to turn yellowish brown and dry out. Rub the seeds off their stems, winnow out the stems and seed covers, thoroughly dry them in filtered light, and store them in airtight jars.

The *adobo* recipe in the recipe section of this book (see page 98) cries out for cumin. Cumin blends well with tomatoes, squash, corn, and beans. Don't be shy about experimenting, but don't be too bold. A little cumin goes a long way, and, like cinnamon, one can quickly tire of it. It is indispensable as a flavor in salsas made with roasted chiles, roasted tomatoes, and roasted garlic. Don't forget to roast the cumin, too, before you add it.

# OREGANO (Orégano)

Authorities on the subject call oregano the most important herb in Mexican cooking. Knowing precisely what to use in a given recipe, however, is difficult because what is called "oregano" in one part of Mexico is different botanically from what is called "oregano" in other parts. In northern Mexico, what is often called *orégano* is the thin leaf of a tough desert plant that has a strong acrid taste and imparts a distinctive flavor to food. In southern Mexico a plant called *oreganón* bears a leaf that looks as if it was meant to be rolled and smoked like a cigar. Yet the taste of southern Mexico's *oreganón* is quite mild.

In the United States, the herb called variously "wild marjoram," "wild oregano," "Greek oregano," and just plain "oregano" is *Origanum vulgare*, the herb that gives the pungent smell and taste associated with Italian spaghetti sauce. *O. vulgare*, a low-growing perennial, is the seed and plant most often sold by nursery and seed companies. Buy it, grow it, and use it with confidence. It may not be the exact same herb called for in your Mexican recipe, but because *O. vulgare* is also used widely in Mexico, no one will accuse you of cooking with less than a Mexican flavor.

## GETTING STARTED

Oregano seed is quite small. To keep from losing seed in a growing medium that is too coarse, screen peat and vermiculite, mixed half and half, into a container that will be well drained, and use the method detailed in Gardening Tips (see page 90) to grow these seeds indoors or outdoors. When the first true leaves develop on the seedlings, use a tooth-

*The Most Mexican of Herbs*

pick to gently separate each seedling from the others, then replant them in a larger container. At maturity, they may be transferred to the open garden.

Provide well-composted, well-drained soil for oregano. Herbs will survive and be useful on poor soil that is poorly watered, but good soil and moisture will produce healthy plants. *O. vulgare* grows bushy up to 30 inches high, and *O. vulgare* Hirta, called Greek oregano, tends to be a sprawling plant. Both like a sunny spot in the garden. *O. vulgare* has oval, dark green leaves and lavender-pink blossoms on spikelike clusters. To get a faster growth of usable oregano, take root divisions from established plants and transfer them to your garden.

## KEEPING IT GOING

Keep oregano in bounds by pinching back growing tips six weeks after planting in the garden. Pinching causes the plants to grow bushier and restrains sprawling Greek oregano from getting out of bounds. No fertilizer is necessary if the bed was prepared with a good application of compost. On sandy, poor soil, give oregano a feeding of manure tea or fish emulsion every six weeks.

## PESTS AND DISEASES

Whiteflies and aphids attack even aromatic herbs. Washing them off with a jet of water early in the morning keeps them from endangering the growth of the plants.

## HARVESTING

Use the fresh leaves of oregano when the plants have produced several growing stems of leaves. To keep from weakening its growth, do not harvest over half of the plant's leaf volume. To prepare the herbs for drying, cut the woody stems of oregano just before the plants go into flower, and hang the stems in an airy, shady place. Protect them from getting dusty by covering them with something as simple as a paper bag. Laying them on a nylon window screen in a hot attic during the summer will quickly desiccate them. Strip the leaves from the stems when they are dry and store them in a bottle with a tightly fitting lid.

No *vinagretta*—a sauce made of oil, vinegar, salt, and pepper—is complete without oregano. *Vinagretta* brings interest to rough salads of tomatoes and cucumbers and lightly cooked side dishes of summer squash and snap beans. Anything served hot with a cooked sauce of tomato, onion, and chile is called ranch style, and oregano is an essential ingredient in this kind of sauce.

*The Most Mexican of Herbs*

# MEXICAN TEA (*Epazote*)

Since Mexican food has taken hold in this country, all the old English names of this common weed have been displaced in favor of its Mexican name, *epazote*. Nowadays, *epazote* is a name used more frequently than Mexican tea or wormseed, but just in case there is some confusion when you attempt to buy it, look for its botanical name, *Chenopodium ambrosioides*. It is a short-lived annual that cannot tolerate cold weather. It will therefore die back every winter, but it will reseed itself to the point that some gardeners consider it a weedy pest. No Mexican gardener would ever eradicate it from the garden, just as no Mexican cook would ever think of cooking a pot of beans without it.

## GETTING STARTED

One or two *epazote* plants will do nicely for a family of four. Few gardeners need all the seeds that come in a packet. Many seed companies offer *epazote* seeds and some nurseries in the Southwest have bedding plants for sale. Early in the spring, plant the seeds in potting soil in containers with good drainage. Keep the containers in filtered sunlight, and keep them moist. Be patient. *Epazote* does

*Mexican Tea*

not germinate quickly. The seedlings should show within two weeks.

## KEEPING IT GOING

When the *epazote* plants are 2 to 4 inches tall, transfer them to the open garden in full sun. They grow to about 36 inches tall and 20 inches wide on good ground, so give them room to expand. *Epazote* will tolerate just about any kind of soil and drought conditions, but good soil and adequate moisture develop the best leaves.

## PESTS AND DISEASES

*Epazote* is a common weed in America and, like many weeds, does not seem to have insect enemies. If insects attack, spray with insecticidal soap.

## HARVESTING

Cut stems from the plant to get the strongly aromatic leaves when the plant is over 6 inches tall. Cuts made from the center stem cause side branching and a more bushy shape to the plant. The fresh leaves give the most flavor, but cut branches and hang them to dry at the end of the season. Strip the *epazote* leaves from the dried stems and store them in an airtight glass jar.

Use the leaves and stems for flavoring in fresh or cooked dishes. The classic combination is *epazote* in black bean recipes, where its job is to bring flavor to the dish and to eliminate flatulence caused by the beans. The flavor of this most Mexican herb is not only indispensable in black bean dishes but also goes well with meats, fish, cheese, corn, and other vegetables.

*The Most Mexican of Herbs*

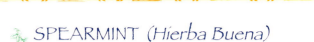

# SPEARMINT (*Hierba Buena*)

*Mentha spicata*, the botanical name for a number of mint varieties, is a perennial. With a good mulch, mint will make it through the winter to return with the same vigor in the spring. There are several kinds of mint, with a surprising number of different odors. There are ginger, pineapple, and peppermints, to name just a few. All are useful as culinary herbs, but spearmint is the "good herb," the *hierba buena* of Mexico. Used most often as a tea to aid digestion, it makes an infrequent appearance in some dishes—chicken, meatballs, salads.

## GETTING STARTED

Mint is easy to grow from seed and easier still if started by root divisions taken from established plants. Prepare a bed in that area of the garden that receives sun during only part of the day. Add compost, dig the soil deeply, and give the surface a fine texture with a garden rake. Broadcast the seed on the surface of the bed and tamp down the seed with the back of the rake. Keep the bed moist until the seedlings appear. After the third and fourth leaves develop, thin the mint to 8- or 12-inch centers. Of course, mint can be also grown in containers and transferred to the open garden later.

## KEEPING IT GOING

When starting mint, the main thing to keep in mind is that it grows so easily and spreads so quickly that it can become a garden pest. Plan some way to limit the spread of the underground rooting stems. One of the best ground-level containers is a large drain tile upended, buried down 6 inches from the top, with the mint confined within its walls. To keep growth fresh and to revitalize the mint patch, use a spade to make a few chops into the root mass. The breaks in the rhysomes will sprout new healthy mint. Reward mint every autumn with composted manure laid on as a winter mulch.

## PESTS AND DISEASES

All mints are robust and thrive under most conditions if their roots are kept moist. Spearmint is relatively free of pests and diseases. Rust can cause reddish-brown spots on the leaves. Cut back and throw away all the rust-affected stems, and water only in the morning hours to avoid conditions that favor rust and other fungi. Mint is occasionally afflicted by other fungal spores, which cause dark spots on the bright green leaves. Try spraying with diluted fish emulsion when the first signs of fungus appears. If fish emulsion does not clear up the problem, spray with a liquid sulfur solution.

## HARVESTING

Take cuttings of mint when the stems are large enough to use. As long as it receives moisture, it thrives on being trimmed and cut. Use only the tender, growing tips for salads and tea. To dry them for the winter, cut woody stems before the flowers blossom, hang them to dry in a well-

*The Most Mexican of Herbs*

ventilated, shady place, and store the stripped leaves in an airtight container.

The best tea is made from an infusion of mint leaves, the tender tips cut fresh from the garden. Use three to five growing tips of leaves per cup of tea; pour hot water over the leaves and allow to steep for 5 minutes. Once you've had a cup of fresh-from-the-garden mint tea, you'll never buy another sack of that dried grassy stuff sold in stores.

# PARSLEY (Perejil)

Parsley is a native of southern Europe, but Mexicans appreciate its rich color, its sprightly taste, and its relatively high content of vitamin C, iron, iodine, and magnesium. Curly-leaf parsley favored in the United States as a garnish to enliven the presentation of food also turns up in Mexico, mostly in places that cater to tourists. For the kitchen garden, however, Mexicans prefer flat-leaf parsley for its superior taste and appearance.

## GETTING STARTED

*Petroselinum crispum* is a biennial that needs to be planted more often than every two years. In warm-weather gardening zones, start parsley in late winter and late summer to keep a crop outside the kitchen door all year round. Parsley tends to go to seed at the end of six months of growth, and sometimes hot or cold weather causes it to bolt. Prepare a bed fertilized with your best compost and manure. When using fresh manure, dig it in and thoroughly mix it with the soil two or three weeks before planting parsley, either the seeds or the transplants.

In sandy soil, cover seeds ½-inch deep and in clay soil, cover them ¼-inch deep. Start seed by sowing directly in the garden or in small cells of good potting mix from which they can be transferred later to the garden. Parsley seed is slow to germinate. Seeds soaked in warm water for a few hours before planting seem to germinate faster. Even though parsley is in the carrot family and, like other members of that family, has a long taproot, it transfers well if not kept too long in small containers.

*The Most Mexican of Herbs*

Keep the seedlings well watered. Lack of moisture in the early stage of growth is the most common reason for inferior older plants. When you're planting in the open garden during hot months, cover the bed with a sheet of plywood to hold moisture at the soil surface and help the seeds germinate. Elevate the plywood with bricks to keep it from contact with the soil and from making a home for slugs and sow bugs. When the first seedlings appear, remove the covering.

## KEEPING IT GOING

Parsley occupies the ground for a long time. To keep it green and producing healthy centers of growth, feed it every two weeks with manure tea or fish emulsion. Side-dress the plants with blood meal every month to produce long, leafy stems. Flat-leafed parsley should be about 18 inches tall if fed and watered properly. Keep it weeded and watered to prolong its growth cycle.

Before cold weather comes, lift a few parsley plants and pot them for use indoors at the kitchen window. Heavy mulches will protect parsley from cold in mild-winter areas. Start another crop indoors six to eight weeks before the last spring frost, and transplant them, after hardening off, to the garden when the ground is workable.

## PESTS AND DISEASES

Whiteflies, carrot rust flies, and cabbage loopers are frequent pests but seldom fatal to the crop. A good stand of parsley on well-manured ground with adequate water should resist most pests and diseases.

## HARVESTING

Cut the outside leaves from the plants when they have become large enough for use. As long as the center of the plant is not cut, parsley should be a cut-and-come-again crop for the period of its growth cycle. Do not throw away the stems in favor of the leaves. The stems have much flavor and provide roughage for the diet. Drying parsley leaves in a dehydrator is practical, but maintaining a round-the-year growth in the garden is not difficult for gardeners in the warmer parts of the United States. Where harsh winters make year-round parsley impractical, harvest the whole crop in the fall. Wash and chop the leaves and stems, seal in plastic bags, and freeze for use through the winter months.

Mexicans like a garnish of finely chopped parsley over chicken, meat, fish, and eggs. Flecks of red chiles and chopped parsley elevate the taste and "Mexicanize" the universal meatball.

*The Most Mexican of Herbs*

# PURSLANE *(Verdolaga)*

Another native of Europe and Asia that has taken hold in Mexico, *Portulaca oleracea* is a low-growing annual potherb. It naturalizes so easily and thrives in such poor soil that most United States gardeners who notice it at all think of it as a pernicious weed. In the Southwest, Mexican workers pick it where they find it, usually growing naturally at the edges of fields and vacant lots. From this humble use it has acquired the name of "Mexican spinach" in the southwestern United States. Considering how highly regarded purslane is in Europe and Asia, it is strange that we do not use it more. Perhaps the mucilaginous texture of purslane, somewhat like okra, is why it is not popular here. A few leaves, stripped from the more succulent stems and mixed with tomatoes and lettuce fresh from the garden, make a Mexican summer salad that should please every lover of fresh greens.

The plant has two main forms: one—a commonly recognized weed—is low growing, with reddish stems and small, dark green, spoon-shaped leaves. The other—more cultivated in gardens and very popular in France and Italy—has large golden-green leaves on yellowish stems and grows more upright. The fleshy leaves and stems are both eaten cooked, but the agreeably acidic taste is best when used fresh in salads. On both the wild and the cultivated purslane, tiny yellow flowers appear at the end of the succulent stems, and after the flowers blossom, green seedpods develop. Once these seedpods have formed, the plant will reseed itself, taking its energy from the fleshy stems, even if it is uprooted. The seeds are as small as grains of dirt, but they are extremely hardy and lie in the soil ready to germinate when the soil warms up next spring.

## GETTING STARTED

The ability of the average United States family to use much purslane is probably limited. I recommend planting the French variety in a small area—about as large as a small coffee table—for your first trial. Purslane will survive and multiply on the poorest soil with little water. To get the best from your efforts, choose a sunny spot in the garden, and compost or manure the soil a week before sowing the seed. Even though transplants of purslane are possible, it grows so rapidly that growing it in one spot seems the most efficient method. Broadcast the seed thinly over the bed after it has been raked smooth to catch the fine seed. Keep damp until the seedlings appear. After the seedlings are established, water as necessary to keep the bed moist. Clay soil needs less watering than sandy soil.

## KEEPING IT GOING

No further fertilizing is necessary after the first preparations. No thinning is necessary to improve the crop. Keep competing weeds out, and start another crop in three or four weeks.

*The Most Mexican of Herbs*

## PESTS AND DISEASES

Purslane is neither attractive to many pests nor is it, in my experience, afflicted by many diseases. Leaf miners may become a problem. The leaf miner fly deposits eggs on the leaf, where the larvae hatch and eat until they are ready to pupate, at which time they fall from the leaf and enter the soil to continue their life cycle. The best way to break the cycle is to pinch off and destroy the leaves when they first show damage from the maggots inside them.

## HARVESTING

Take thinnings for the kitchen as soon as the plants are large enough to use. These first thinnings are tender and give the pleasantly acidic taste of purslane to salads and garnishes. At about the third week, the plants are large enough to cut stems for cooking in recipes for spinach and chard. Try stir-frying a bunch in a little oil with some red and green chiles for a lunch of *burritos con verdolagas*. Six weeks from germination, the entire crop will show signs of declining, the stems will become tough, flowers will appear, and the seedpods will develop. Pull the failing plants up by the roots and leave them in areas where you want purslane to sprout next year. The plant's seed pods will burst and sow next year's crop.

# GARDENING TIPS

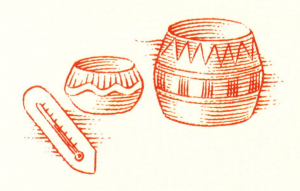

## START TOMATO, PEPPER, AND HERB SEEDS INDOORS

Several kinds of vegetables and herbs need to be started early to take full advantage of the growing season. Tomatoes and peppers, in particular, need to be started early, eight to ten weeks before the last frost.

Only a few basic items are needed:

- a sunny windowsill
- an inexpensive drugstore hot pad
- a thermometer
- a few containers
- a growing medium free of plant diseases
- a clear plastic cover

Less necessary, but useful to have, is a daylight spectrum light to keep the seedlings from becoming too leggy as they reach for light.

The two most common starting problems are failure to germinate and damping-off. A cool growing medium most frequently causes seed failure. Bottom warmth provided by a heating pad prevents seeds from rotting and gives them that extra push warm-weather plants need. Damping-off is caused by a fungus that spreads across the surface of the soil and strangles the seedlings. Damping-off is easily prevented by using peat moss and vermiculite, available at garden shops. Mix the peat and vermiculite half-and-half, and push the tomato and pepper seeds about a ¼-inch down into it. Do not attempt to cover fine seed—oregano, for example. Just scatter them across the surface of the peat–vermiculite mixture and carefully water the containers from below.

Cover the container with clear plastic refrigerator wrap to keep the growing medium moist. When the seeds begin to germinate, remove the plastic wrap. Clear plastic covers that cover bakeshop goods work even better than plastic wrap. Containers made of thin plastic with individual cells and clear plastic covers, essentially mini-greenhouses, are available from gardening supply stores.

Watering seedlings from the bottom of the container is important to keep from disturbing the seeds and to avoid damping-off. Place the holding tray on top of a drugstore heating pad. An inexpensive thermometer will help regulate the temperature. Tomato seeds germinate well at 70° to 80°F. Peppers need a warmer setting, from 75° to 85°F.

Tomato seeds germinate within a week to ten days. Peppers usually take longer. Some tiny herb and flower seeds may take more than ten days to germinate. When most of the seedlings are up, remove the clear plastic cover and turn the heating pad off. In cold zones, it might be advisable to turn on the heating pad at night.

When the seedlings develop leaves beyond the first two immature leaves, carefully remove the seedlings from the vermiculite–peat mixture and pot them in a good potting soil. Keep these small pots of seedlings on bottom heat if the weather is cold during the day. If possible, move them outside, under the protection of a plastic cover on cold days and nights, and harden them off.

## IMPROVING THE SOIL WITH COMPOST

We can always improve the quality of our soil, and every year that we garden we should be working to this end. The single most important job beyond digging itself is adding compost to the soil. Compost is made up of organic materials that have been broken down by bacteria and other organisms. Working compost into the soil alters its structure and improves fertility. The two basic types of soil structure are sand and clay. Sandy soils allow water to penetrate easily to get to plants' roots, but sandy soil quickly loses moisture to the atmosphere and allows water to drain past the roots. Compost added to sandy soil gives water molecules something to hold on to, keeping moisture in the root zone. As compost continues to decompose, it gives up vital chemicals to nourish the plants.

To simplify a subject often made complicated, successful compost piles need follow only a few elementary rules: **Keep the stuff small** (for example, chop the weeds into 6-inch pieces), **keep the stuff damp** (wet it down initially and cover it with a plastic sheet), and **keep the stuff stirred up** (use a garden fork to turn it over periodically). Break any of the three elementary rules and it will take more time to make finished compost, but even unfinished compost is usable in the garden if dug in several weeks before planting.

# APPENDIXES

# RECIPES FOR THE
# MEXICAN KITCHEN GARDEN

Although suggestions for preparing vegetables appear with the gardening instructions, some vegetables need more specific directions to prepare them in the Mexican style. Some of the recipes are no more complicated than giving a peanut butter sandwich a Mexican twist by adding a few chiles (not a bad idea, come to think of it—try a pinch of sugar and a toasted Anaheim).

# BEANS

## Frijoles de Olla (Pot Beans)

2 cups dried beans (pinto, tan, white, or black)
1 garlic clove lightly crushed
¼ white onion chopped coarsely
water to cover
salt to taste

Sort through the dried beans on a surface that allows you to see and pick out pieces of dirt and small stones. Wash the cleaned beans in two changes of cold water. Beans older than one year benefit from soaking in cold water for one or two hours. Overnight soaking is unnecessary. Use the soaking water as the liquid in which to cook the beans. Always begin cooking dried beans in cold water. Put all the ingredients in a pot and cover with water. Use a pot that has a lid that allows some of the steam to escape. Never salt the beans until they are finished cooking. Bring the water to a boil and then adjust to a simmer. Cook the beans until tender by testing to see if they are cooked through. Depending on the size and age of the beans, cooking time can vary from 1 to 3 hours. If too much liquid is lost during the cooking, add more water. The goal is to have tender beans that hold their shape in a delicious beany syrup.

*Serves 4 to 6.*

**Variation:** When using black beans, add three or four sprigs of *epazote* to the pot during the last ten minutes of simmering.

# CACTUS

## Nopalitos (Chopped Cactus Pads)

3 tablespoons vegetable oil

4 garlic cloves, peeled and chopped

3 green onion tops, coarsely chopped

1 pound of *nopalitos* (cactus pads), coarsely chopped

3 green onion bottoms, coarsely chopped

¼ cup Anaheim green chiles, sliced in thick strips, seeds and stems removed

¼ cup hot or sweet red chiles, sliced in thick strips. seeds and stems removed

salt to taste

Heat the oil in a heavy pan. Add the garlic and the green onion tops to the oil, and braise just long enough to wilt the tops and make the garlic transparent. Add the *nopalitos*, stirring continuously until they give up their liquid (about ten minutes). The liquid that comes from cactus has an okra-like, mucilaginous texture that some do not like. Onion tops and the reduction of the liquid will eliminate this sliminess. Remove all the *nopalitos* and onion tops with a slotted spoon, leaving only the liquid in the pan. Reduce the liquid further, but do not allow it to burn. When the liquid has thickened, add the *nopalitos*, the green onion bottoms, the chiles, and salt, and cook the cactus until it is tender and the pieces have an oily sheen. Serve on lettuce leaves and top with a rosette of radish and a wedge of lime.

*Serves 4.*

**Variations:** Serve with coarsely chopped *epazote* leaves and grated cheese, or serve with a sprinkling of whole pine nuts.

# CHILES

## Adobo de Chile Colorado (Red Chile Marinade)

- 12 dried pods of mild red chile—ancho, mulato, or colorado
- ½ cup water
- ¼ cup vinegar
- 2 tablespoons balsamic vinegar
- ½ cup olive oil
- 1 medium onion, coarsely chopped
- 4 whole garlic cloves, peeled
- 2 whole spice cloves
- ½ tablespoon dry Mexican oregano leaves
- ½ tablespoon of cumin
- ½ stick *canela* (Mexican cinnamon)
- ¼ cup brown sugar
- salt to taste

Carefully toast the chile pods by turning them a few seconds on each side on a griddle or grill, or in a skillet. Chiles burn easily, and burned chiles spoil the *adobo*. If burned, throw them out. Soak the toasted chiles in enough hot water to cover them for 30 minutes. To reduce the amount of spicy heat from the *adobo*, remove stems and seeds from the softened chile pods. For more heat, include the seeds. Add ½ cup of the water in which the chiles soaked to the rest of the ingredients and purée everything in a blender or food processor.

Use as a barbecue sauce for meat, chicken, or fish. Use also as a base for chile con carne and other sauces. Refrigerate for up to a month or freeze for longer periods.

*Makes approximately 1 quart.*

# CORN

## Sopa de Maíz (Corn Soup)

1 tablespoon of butter
½ white onion, coarsely chopped
8 cups fresh corn kernels sliced off the cob (about 10
   ears)
6 cups canned chicken broth
6 half breasts of chicken, grilled and shredded by hand
4 Anaheim, New Mexico, or *poblano* green chiles,
   skinned, seeded, deveined, and chopped fine
1 tablespoon oregano
4 cloves garlic, crushed and minced
1 cup summer squash (zucchini or yellow), chopped fine
salt to taste
1 cup shredded *añejo* or mozzarella cheese
1 cup cilantro, chopped fine

Put the butter and onion into a pot large enough for finishing the soup. Stir continuously until just before the onion begins to become transparent. Add the corn and continue stirring until the corn begins to cook. Add the chicken broth, chicken breasts, chiles, oregano, and garlic. Bring the pot to a boil and adjust to simmer for 5 minutes. Taste for salt and add if needed. Add the summer squash and simmer until the squash is cooked but still has color and is firm.

Ladle into bowls and sprinkle the cheese on top. Sprinkle the cilantro on top of the cheese and serve.

*Serves 4 to 6.*

# SQUASH

## Calabacitas con Queso
## (Summer Squash with Cheese)

6 small summer squash
1 chile (choose an Anaheim type for mild heat or serrano for more heat)
1 tablespoon of butter or vegetable oil
¼ cup of grated Parmesan or *queso añejo* (aged cheese)
½ lime
salt to taste

After removing the stems and flower scars from each end of the summer squash, split them in half lengthwise. Slash the cut surfaces and arrange them in a baking pan with the cut side up. Butter and salt them. If using an Anaheim-type chile, toast it to remove the skin from the flesh, and take out the seeds and veins. If using a hotter, thin-skinned variety such as serrano, merely take out the seeds and veins. Slice the chile lengthwise in julienne strips and place the strips on top of the squash. Bake the squash until it is almost cooked but still has shape. Sprinkle the grated cheese over the chiles and squash and return the squash to the oven to brown the cheese topping. Right before serving, give each squash a few drops of lime juice.

*Serves 4.*

# TOMATILLOS

## Salsa *Verde* (Green Hot Sauce)

1 pound (10 to 20) *tomatillos*
¼ cup fresh green Anaheim chiles, seeds and stems
    removed, for mild salsa, or for spicy hot salsa, ¼ cup
    jalapeño or serrano chiles
¼ cup fresh cilantro, chopped fine
½ cup white onion, chopped fine
2 garlic cloves, peeled and chopped fine
1 tablespoon lime juice
⅛ teaspoon sugar
salt to taste

Remove the stems and husks from the *tomatillos*, quarter them, and finely chop them. Cook them in a covered pan, stirring occasionally until they reach the thickness of sauce. As they cook, they take on a gelatinous sheen, the sign that the cooking stage has finished. Combine the *tomatillos* in a large bowl with all the other ingredients and mix thoroughly. The gelatin-like consistency of *tomatillo* and the tiny seeds within the sauce are the marks of genuine *salsa verde*. These marks and *tomatillo's* superior taste are why green tomatoes are not an adequate substitute. Refrigerate for a few days or freeze for longer periods.

    *Makes approximately 1 quart.*

# TOMATOES

## Salsa Fresca
## (Uncooked Tomato Hot Sauce)

1 cup ripe tomatoes, unpeeled and chopped fine
½ cup white onion, chopped fine
4 to 8 chiles (habaneros, serranos, or jalapeños, depending on the amount of heat wanted), chopped fine
2 garlic cloves, peeled and chopped fine
¼ cup flat-leafed parsley, chopped fine
¼ cup cilantro, chopped fine
lime juice to taste
salt to taste

Mix thoroughly tomatoes, onion, chiles, garlic, parsley, cilantro, salt, and lime juice. If tomatoes are red ripe, no additional liquid is necessary. If they are less than juicy, add ice water to bring the mixture to the consistency of a sauce. This sauce does not keep well in the refrigerator or the freezer. Use freshly made on chips, tacos, avocado, squash, or scrambled eggs. To preserve, simmer on the stove for 5 minutes, and after cooling, keep in the refrigerator.

*Makes approximately 1 quart.*

**Variation:** Substitute cucumbers for tomatoes.

# DRYING AND STORING HERBS

The best time to collect herbs is just before the plants go into flower. At that period the flavorful oils of *epazote*, oregano, cilantro, parsley, and mint are at their peak. Tradition holds that the best time of the day for collecting herbs is early in the morning, just after the dew has evaporated. Cut herb branches with clippers rather than breaking or pulling them off. When harvesting dried seeds of cilantro and cumin, wait until the seeds turn slightly brown. Wait too long to harvest seeds, and the pods may shatter, scattering the seeds on the ground.

Dry branches of herbs by gathering them in loose bunches, securing each bunch with string at the cut end, and hanging them in an airy, dry place away from sunlight. A garage, an attic, a basement, or another room in the house all serve equally well, as long as the herbs are protected from moisture, stagnant air, and direct sunlight. Laying small quantities of herbs on paper, clean and free of newspaper ink, works if air circulates around them. A vegetable and fruit dehydrator also does a good job.

After the herbs are dry to the touch, store in containers with airtight lids. Light decreases the shelf life of herbs. Containers that are light-tight as well as airtight make the best storage vessels. Most dried herbs are useful for a year.

# SEED AND PLANT SOURCES

The accompanying notes intend to direct the buyer to those vegetables in the Mexican kitchen garden that may not be easily found elsewhere.

**Enchanted Seeds**
P.O. Box 6087
Las Cruces, NM 88006
Specializes in hard-to-get chiles of the Southwest and Mexico.

**J. L. Hudson, Seedsman**
P.O. Box 1058
Redwood City, CA 94064
Mexican cactus, culinary herbs, medicinal herbs, and an excellent variety of Mexican vegetables.

**Johnny's Selected Seeds**
Foss Hill Road
Albion, ME 04910
Amaranth, beans, cilantro, *epazote*, garlic, peppers, pumpkins, squash, and *tomatillo*.

**Mellinger's Inc.**
Dept. MKG
2310 W. South Range Road
North Lima, OH 44452
Amaranth, cilantro, cumin, Indian corn, gourds, jícama, peppers, pumpkins, squash, and *tomatillo*.

**The Pepper Gal**
P.O. Box 23006
Fort Lauderdale, FL 33307
At last count, 167 varieties of hot peppers.

**Pinetree Garden Seeds**
Box 300
New Gloucester, ME 04260
Beans, bolt-resistant cilantro, squash, Indian corn, *epazote*, herbs, jícama, peppers, and pumpkins.

**Plants of the Southwest**
Agua Fria, Rt. 6 Box 11A
Santa Fe, NM 87501
Two kinds of amaranth,
many beans, cilantro, Indian
corn, *epazote*, peppers, squash,
and *tomatillo*.

**Territorial Seed Co.**
P.O. Box 157
Cottage Grove, OR 97424
Cilantro, Indian corn, *epazote*,
five kinds of garlic, peppers,
purslane, squash, and *tomatillos*.

**Tomato Growers' Supply**
P. O. Box 2237
Fort Myers, FL 33902
The last stop for tomato
seed. Also a good selection
of hot peppers.

# FURTHER READING

Bradley, Fern Marshall, and Barbara W. Ellis. *The Organic Gardener's Handbook of Natural Insect and Disease Control.* Emmaus, Pennsylvania: Rodale Press, 1992. Recommended for its excellent color plates of pests and diseases and for its common-sense methods of combating them.

DeWitt, Dave, and Nancy Gerlach. *The Whole Chile Pepper Book.* Boston: Little, Brown, 1990. Does not limit its focus to, but has good background information on, chiles as they are used in Mexico and the Southwest.

Kennedy, Diana. *The Art of Mexican Cooking: Traditional Mexican Cooking for Aficionados.* New York: Bantam Books, 1989. If we had only one book on the subject, this one, by the Mexican equivalent of Julia Child, should be it.

# ACKNOWLEDGMENTS

I am indebted to several people from whom I received much help. My thanks to Maximo Contín for his comments on the manuscript. My thanks to Stuart Blumberg, a dear friend of many years, whose careful reading of the text and helpful suggestions made this a more readable book. I am greatly indebted to M. C. Goldman, formerly the executive editor of *Organic Gardening* magazine. Without Lee Goldman's encouragement and support for many years, this book would not have been written. Finally, I acknowledge a debt of gratitude to the many Mexicans, too numerous to name, who have been my unselfish teachers, my patient students, and my beloved friends.

# ABOUT THE AUTHOR

John Meeker has been a garden writer for more than thirty years, having written and sold hundreds of gardening articles. He is presently the Western Advisor to Rodale's *Organic Gardening* magazine. He has contributed to various books published by Rodale Press, most significantly *Unusual Vegetables*, which like this book, gave him the opportunity to write about his ethnic favorites, vegetable off-beats, and the culinary unconventional. In a lifetime of gardening flowers and vegetables, the sizes of his gardens have varied from a 24-inch driveway strip to a half acre, and he is not satisfied with each year's garden unless something new and different is growing there.